FEB 6 1987

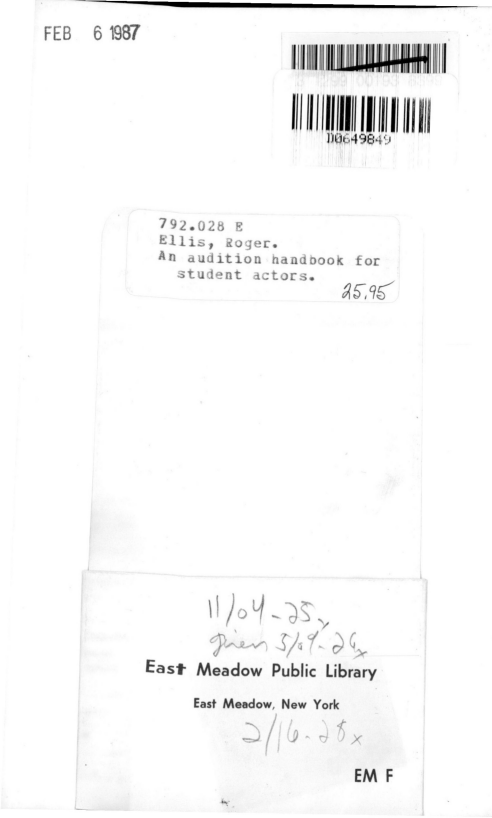

East Meadow Public Library

East Meadow, New York

EM F

An Audition Handbook for Student Actors

The actor must have the soul of a fairy and the hide of a walrus.—*William Redfield, actor*

Just get out there and kick-ass!—*Robert Goldsby, producer-director*

When you're working-up an audition always keep one thing in mind: "Would you ask people to pay money to see that?"—*Aaron Frankel, director*

Roger Ellis

An Audition Handbook for Student Actors

Nelson-Hall Publishers **nh** Chicago

Library of Congress Cataloging in Publication Data

Ellis, Roger.
   An audition handbook for student actors.

   Bibliography: p.
   Includes index.
   1. Acting—Auditions. I. Title.
PN2071.A92E45   1985   792'.028   85-8868
ISBN 0-8304-1017-1 (cloth)
ISBN 0-8304-1157-7 (paper)

Manufactured in the United States of America

10 9 8 7 6 5 4 3 2 1

The paper in this book is pH neutral (acid-free).

For *Mary, Zan, Karen* and *Jeremiah*

Contents

Acting Exercises

Acknowledgments

Among the many people who helped me with this handbook—and who are still helpful to me when I visit them in their studios or attend their shows—I'd like to especially thank a few whose contributions have been particularly valuable. These include Bob Goldsby and Angela Paton of the Berkeley Stage Company, Jim Panowski of Northern Michigan University, Jane Armitage of the Drama Studio/London, William Oliver of the University of California at Berkeley, and New York director Aaron Frankel, all of whom cheerfully gave me hours of their time in conversation and manuscript preparation. I also want to thank Tim Carhart and Jane Brody of Chicago's "Audition Centre," Jane Alderman from the Goodman School, and Jack Fletcher of A.C.T., whose approaches to the training of young actors were especially valuable. Cynthia Auerbach of the Chautauqua Opera Festival and Bob Peterson, opera producer, were extremely cordial and helpful to me in preparing the chapter on musical theatre. The Scholarly Research and Development Committee at Grand Valley State College gave me generous financial assistance from the outset of this project. Lastly, I'm certain that the insights of many nameless but memorable actors and students whose performances have passed before my eyes over the years are also contained somewhere in the pages of this book.

Chapter one

Introduction

Somewhere along the line, every young actor encounters that puzzling statement about learning the craft of his profession: "Acting is a gift, a talent, something that can't be taught." And it's certainly true—as anyone involved with acting training realizes—that without some innate ability to play and to project oneself into imaginary circumstances, nothing that is ever done in the studio will make an actor out of someone who is not. On the other hand, what *can* be taught in studio is technique, which is also important. Without a method to his madness, the gifted student is left without a direction for his energy, a form according to which his creative impulses can be *productively* channeled.

I think it's necessary for acting students to keep this point in mind during training, because no one can "teach" you how to act, nor can anyone teach you how to audition and get a role. If you have the talent, though, you *can* channel it and make it work better for you. Your instructors and coaches can introduce you to certain techniques. They can encourage you to develop what talent you have by giving you a framework in which you can test and challenge yourself. A good acting or auditioning class (the two are inseparably related) can provide an environment in which you can explore basic methods that might work for you as a person who is different from everyone else. Expressive movement, vocal flexibility, character motivation, sensitivity to language, familiarity with period conventions—these are areas that acting students explore in order to apply their abilities to the complex and *practical*

1

demands of stage performance. The technique of how to get there in the first place—how to audition well—is another essential area that should be developed as early as possible and continually refined as your acting matures.

When you perform in plays and study acting in a collegiate setting, there are advantages and drawbacks that you should be aware of. On the plus side is the fact that you're in an excellent situation for learning about the profession. Here in the United States, the major training grounds for stage careers are the university and college drama programs. Whether or not a student stays long enough to earn a degree before entering professional training is unimportant. For most actors, first contact with the tools of the trade will likely come from studying in college classrooms, auditioning for and acting in college productions, and following a study plan, which in many places can amount to a sound preprofessional program in performing arts.[1]

But a collegiate environment does not always encourage students to fully develop their talents, and this is especially true when it comes to audition situations. A major trap of the college campus for student actors is that they'll be working with others whose commitment to excellence, whose need to get onstage and perform well is in many cases less intense, less insistent than their own. It is this commitment that distinguishes the amateur from the professional in all fields. You will probably sense this most keenly every time you try out for a role in a campus show.

As an acting student, remember that many other college students perform only out of curiosity about acting, or out of a general desire to participate in some lively extracurricular group activity, or out of a vaguely defined need for personal enrichment and self-growth. These are all good purposes in themselves and a necessary part of the collegiate environment, but they are useless when it comes to doing a good audition. In fact, everywhere you turn, you may feel yourself up against collegiate attitudes that foster complacency: the protective environment that often makes training and production experience available to everyone, the grades which seem to "validate" your progress if you simply complete the requirements, or teacher-directors who have gotten used to tolerating instructional and performance mediocrity. In all such cases, your motivation for competing and for selling yourself, which good acting and good auditioning require, is absent or even stifled. And no actor has ever made it without learning how to carry off these cornerstones of the profession.

Competition, then, is a basic challenge that acting students have to be able to master and even enjoy! You should regard auditioning not as a dreaded and embarrassing necessity, but instead as one of the best ways of giving a truly satisfying stage performance and of learning your strengths and weaknesses as an actor. The one-shot nature of tryouts, in fact, is really an asset because it forces you to focus all your energy and skill into those few brief minutes when the director will size you up and decide upon your ability to play the part. Like a scene in a play, you get only one chance to perform an audition, and then it's gone. So it's a great opportunity to show what you've got, but an audition is never easy to handle. You'll be hustled onstage alone, or with a few others, to read a scene. The judgmental eyes of the director will compare you with others who've gone before and with the demands of the role. And all the while that distracting, insistent question will pop into your head: How can the director possibly know what I can do just by throwing me up on stage for a few hectic minutes like this?

Well, the answer to that is that the director can't know, and it isn't really necessary that he or she should. The first lesson to learn about auditioning is this: just what are you there for? *The auditors will know about you only what you can show them in those few minutes, only those specific talents you display and your manner of presenting yourself.* Both are equally important and there's nothing else to be considered. This businesslike attitude is something I was never taught in my educational or professional training. After I'd learned it, the whole audition process became much more sensible and less threatening to me. After all, why should a director bother with the details of classes I've taken, how much I really want to play a part, or what famous actors I admire on film or TV any more than I should care about his personal artistic growth or directorial experience? The task at hand is a specific play with particular demands, and all that *really* matters on both sides of the casting table is whether or not the auditionee can display the skills and the flexibility that the part requires. No more, no less is necessary. *The problem thus reduces itself to a single question for you: How can I show the auditors my range of skills for a given play and let them know that I'm capable of learning more?*

I think if student actors begin at this point, if they remember that they're presenting and selling themselves as talent when they prepare for tryouts, they'll be aggressive and sensitive to the text and be miles ahead of so many others who really have no anchor to ground them when they plunge into that highly competitive situation vaguely hoping for the best. From the director's standpoint, it is the actor with confidence and focus, the performer who has shaped the audition piece in order to sell his or her talents (even if it is shaped somewhat incorrectly) who stands out from the others—the succession of uncertain attempts, murky interpretations, improvisational flashes-in-pans, and reluctant, fearful readings that pass deadeningly before the director's eyes. Remember that no one is going to beat a path to your door. You must sell the package to them, and you must stand out and "advertise" yourself in your audition. As director Doug Johnson of the old Stanford Repertory Theatre once advised me, "You want to leave those auditions people with a little nugget, a little gem that's polished and complete, so they'll be able to pick you out of the crowd when they cast."

This handbook is about fashioning that package, the four-to-six minute "hard sell" to the director. I'm not talking about distorting the script in order to simply line up your "techniques" like canned goods on a supermarket shelf. Leave that sort of thing to your fellow students in computers or accounting where no personal purchase, no individual creativity is required when they seek work. As an acting student, you'll need to draw on everything you've learned onstage and in studio and apply it to the audition at hand when you fashion your tryout "package." You may have spent ten weeks in a theory class investigating the structure of Shakespeare's *Lear*, but at tryouts you may be expected only to recognize and to play the key structural points in one scene by Ibsen—and that may be the only chance you have to do it. You might have read poetry for three months in an oral interpretation class, but when the director asks you to try a scene from Edward Albee's *Zoo Story*, he or she will be concerned only with the way you can phrase, punctuate, and build one short speech. What may have seemed academic in a drama classroom suddenly becomes nuts and bolts for you at tryouts. But beyond the classroom skills you may have developed, there is also the need to show that you have taken the time to make those skills a part of your personality, of your expressiveness as an actor. As one Chicago-based performer commented, "The best training I've ever gotten is selling refrigerators and color TVs. . . . I'm not saying hustle and be an insurance salesman, but just be yourself because that's what you're selling!"[2] You must use, distill, and focus what you've learned into a short presentation in order to demonstrate that you are equipped to find and play your character's goals, the beats in a scene, or the basic relationships with the other characters. This is what I mean by "selling yourself" at an audition. Think in a businesslike manner.

Obviously, much of your performance can be set beforehand when you work on your own pieces, but there are also techniques you can apply to audition material you've never seen before (cold readings). In this handbook, I've tried to lay out some guidelines for doing good auditions, but you should also keep in mind that there is no sure-fire formula for success in this business. In fact, the actor who "follows the rules" is usually the one who turns out dull performances—technically correct, but lacking spontaneity. Like acting exercises, audition techniques should be studied and rehearsed in a disciplined, systematic fashion, because only then can they sink into your mind and become a working part of the beautifully intuitive process of acting.

In order for this to happen, "technique" and rules must be forgotten. As Martha Graham once remarked about disciplined spontaneity, "Through all times, the acquiring of technique has been for one purpose— so to train the body as to make possible any demand made upon it by that inner self which has the vision of what needs to be said."[3] And Michael Shurtleff, the famous American acting coach, declares at the end of his book on professional auditioning that after studying all his guideposts, the actor should then disregard them and take the improvisational risk of falling flat on his face: "Consistency is the death of good acting. . . . No one is going to hire a frozen robot to do a vivid job of acting."[4]

You should let the same advice apply to your work on the methods explained here: read the handbook closely, drill yourself in applying the basic methods, and then forget them. Rely upon this experience to sensitize you to presenting scenes. You'll certainly find that every audition situation is different, just as each play and its acting demands is different from every other play. No hard-and-fast rules apply in every case. The working professional, of course, has years of stage experience, dozens of roles in many plays and styles which do not *exactly* tell how to read scenes at tryouts but which provide a built-in sensitivity to such things as pacing, turning-points, humor, or character motivation. Stage experience tips an actor off to the performance values in an audition piece just as the approaches contained in this book can help you spot what needs to be done with any audition material you will have to present.

How to use this book

The ideas in this text have evolved out of several years' experience in teaching auditioning skills to college students and in working with theatre professionals around the country. Although I give workshops and coach young professionals on an individual basis, my intention here has been to write a class text for college actors. I strongly feel that acting students should study auditioning for at least ten to fifteen weeks in order to feel confident. At least read a short handbook such as this one which by itself can improve your performance. And I think students should approach this subject early because a good understanding of what auditions are and how to do them well can help to place performance training into perspective.

Unlike many technical skills such as mime, dance, makeup, and fencing, auditioning cannot be effectively learned apart from the overall context of a drama program.

A first-rate audition will depend upon expressive movement, literary analysis, an understanding of dramatic structure, and other skills that are often taught without a clear connection to actual production problems. Thus intensive work on how to make all your training relevant to auditioning and performing can help make you aware of your limitations and strengths and motivate your approach to classroom work in other subjects.

This book tries to provide a complete survey of audition situations that you will most frequently encounter in school. Chapter 2 begins with theory and explains the auditions context in detail so that you can form a healthy competitive attitude towards presenting yourself in public. Underlying this chapter is my belief that ignorance about the auditions situation is the actor's worst enemy. Why auditions are a necessary part of the production process, the various kinds of auditions and what is expected of participants, and the importance of motivating oneself and practicing self-discipline are a few of the chapter's key topics. Chapters 3 through 6 deal with practical approaches toward problems with prepared and unprepared readings. Chapter 7 treats the problems of presenting yourself in resumes and interviews. Chapter 8 ties up the practical approaches developed earlier in the text by assembling the observations of numerous professionals on the subject of auditions.

Although most students will find chapters 3 through 6 most interesting because they deal with the nuts and bolts of problems, the background material in chapter 2 is absolutely necessary and should be studied closely because many of the problems that students have with tryouts can be overcome by forming healthy attitudes towards the situation. For instance, though there are no sure-fire methods for overcoming stage fright, a realistic understanding of what is expected at tryouts and a sense of confidence about the talents one does possess can go far towards reducing the inhibiting feelings of self-consciousness and confusion that always arise. Chapter 2 explains why a positive attitude is necessary and how to begin to form your own. Once that has been established, effective methods can be added for performing a good audition.

There are also three appendices to this handbook. Appendix A contains all the monologues and scenes referred to in the text exercises, either for solo or for class work. None of these should be used for an audition, though, because they're very familiar to directors and can place you at a disadvantage when freshness and originality are being sought. Appendix B contains a variety of sample documents connected with auditioning—tip sheets, resumes, casting notices, and the like—which can help familiarize you with some of the "paperwork" relating to auditions. Appendix C is designed as a handy reference section for students who wish to pursue work beyond the basic level explained here or who are curious about professional acting as a career. Listed in Appendix C are anthologies of scenes and monologues, books describing the acting marketplace, and basic acting texts that were recommended to me by professional and educational theatre people while researching this handbook.

I hope that readers will take away from this handbook an improved sense of self-confidence about doing auditions—something I found difficult to master as an actor. I find that once the dreadful mystique of the situation has disappeared, students eagerly try out for all kinds of plays; I'm grateful when I come to casting that they've been able to shuck off their inhibitions and show me the kinds of things I need to discover about them for the play at hand. Whether or not those things are the "right" ones for the part is not an important consideration for me, because I know I can work with a disciplined student actor to bring out what the part requires (what else are directors for?). And if a beginning student just entering the drama program can gain auditions training and compete aggressively in college-wide tryouts without feeling intimidated by "naturally talented" competitors or "old regulars" in the department, then he's well on the way towards carving-out a place for himself in the production program and, I hope, in the larger field of professional theatre as well.

Chapter two

The Auditions Context

What is an audition? Simply stated, an audition is the most efficient process of choosing actors to perform different roles in a production. The process may involve reading a scene or presenting a monologue, singing, dancing, performing improvisational exercises, having an interview, or demonstrating special or unusual skills. It is normally conducted before a group of individuals called directors or auditors who have the responsibility for casting the show: the stage director, the choreographer, the vocal director, the production stage manager, the producers, and their various assistants. The auditions process can either be "closed"—only the above-mentioned people being present—or "open" to all the other auditionees waiting their turns to try out.[1] Frequently there will be a preliminary session of "general" auditions to separate the most appropriate candidates from many others who, for various reasons, are unsuitable for the play. These will be followed by another session of "callbacks" in order to determine the final choices in casting. A typical college or university general audition may take as long as sixty to ninety minutes (somewhat shorter for nonmusical plays), of which only six to ten minutes may be spent actually performing for the auditors. Professional auditions are considerably shorter. Notification of the auditors' decisions is normally made one or two days after callbacks, although professional groups may delay final casting for several months.

You should bear in mind at all times that general auditions are a very tense and complicated process for the director because most of a play's success is dependent upon proper casting. Many directors point out that the best auditionees are actors who concentrate on where the auditors are coming from, instead of worrying about their own unsteady feelings. Actors often call auditioning a "meat market" or "cattle call." A large number of nervous, excitable people will attend general tryouts (many of them not even actors). They will probably know nothing or very little about the play being cast, each will feel in direct competition with everyone else, and all will be treated more or less impersonally by the people in charge.

At this stage of the action the smartest thing to do is to keep your eye on the director's decision-making process. Pay attention, stay alert, listen to and follow all suggestions and instructions, and perform with a positive, aggressive attitude. Put yourself in the position of the casting people who must carefully scrutinize dozens (or even hundreds) of faces, weigh each person against the demands of the play, and make an irrevocable decision about whether or not an individual has potential that can be developed in a four-to-six-week rehearsal period.

Collegiate tryouts

When you prepare for auditions at your school, there are two special pitfalls you must be sure to avoid. The first is complacency. Remind yourself that all actors must go through the auditions process to get roles, and this for good reasons. On the professional stage, of course, celebrities are often cast without trying out because their talents are well known. But this is certainly not the case with collegiate performers. Even though you may have worked for a particular director before and you may feel your abilities are familiar to the people behind the casting table, remember that they will base their decisions primarily upon how you read *this* time, for *this particular play*. Don't rest on your past triumphs.

Believing yourself to be somehow "favored" at casting because of your association with the directors who are also likely to be your teachers is one of the commonest traps for student actors. Remember that when your teacher sits behind that casting table, he or she has put on another hat and expects quite a different relationship with students in this new, intensely competitive situation.

One auditor and acting coach at Chicago's Goodman Theatre commented that a certain sense of complacency is always in evidence somewhere during auditions, especially with high school or college prima donnas: "There's a self-centeredness there that has got to go away," he remarked. "That's the trouble with being a high school star. Everything has come too easy."[2] Professional actor and director Tom Markus puts this idea in no uncertain terms when he says, "I suppose I'm least patient with students who saunter into an audition ill prepared, mistaking their teacher for their friend and not realizing the teacher has become director and that friendship has nothing to do with the casting of a play. These students (the most talented are frequently the greatest offenders) are teaching themselves very bad work habits. Their teachers are doing them a grievous injury by permitting such poor professional behavior."[3]

Although college directors often choose plays with the skills of their students in mind, very rarely are roles precast. Few directors will tie their hands in advance before knowing all the talent that is available. I've heard many college and university directors comment on how certain kinds of plays— Shakespeare, for example, or musicals—will draw all kinds of talent "out of the woodwork" on campus to perform. Numerous other directors, such as well-known Kabuki director Leonard Pronko from Pomona College in California, prefer to work with students who are not old regulars in the drama program. Why? Because "nonactors" often have natural acting abilities and fresh qualities in their onstage presence that directors can use. Or they can learn new techniques and behave spontaneously without worrying about "finding motivation" or "searching for the character," methods appropriate to the studio but not to performance. Even though you may feel you have lots of training and experience going for you, *never fall into the trap of only half-trying at an audition,* no matter what your experience might be. You are trying out for every role in that play; you are in serious competition with everyone else at the auditions.

Bear in mind the fact that all auditions are important to you. *Audition for every play that comes along, every chance you get.* This too is a common trap for young actors: judging the play or the roles in advance, deciding they are not "right" for certain parts, or the play is not for them. The only thing that should enter into consideration is whether or not you are willing to devote the time to the project.

I am constantly amazed by student actors' inability to read a play creatively and to examine an audition piece as a blueprint for performance possibilities, despite the amount of training they have in theatre classes. We intellectualize our response and short-circuit the rest of our organism instead of asking the important question: What can be vividly played in this scene when I get up there? Too often the student is thinking, "I hope I get it right when I get up there." Nothing is ever inherently "right" about a scene on the page. What is "right" is what the actor and director settle upon as an interpretation or as an objective to play. In an audition, *you* choose what is right, *you* find the objective (whatever it is), and you play it fully.

Trust the director. Remind yourself that 99 percent of what a role contains will never occur to you until opening night *after* you have explored the part for dozens of hours in rehearsals and discover what works with that audience. If you decide in advance that one part is "right" for you and another isn't, you've closed a lot of doors that could lead you to getting cast. Michael Shurtleff put it well when he advised, "I think an actor should audition every damn chance he gets. If you're twenty-three and blond and you get a chance to audition for an eighty-year-old, brunette grandmother, go and audition . . . read for anything where anyone will allow you to read. You need the practice."[4]

Shurtleff's advice concerns not only the major stage productions your school may be doing, but also student productions that are usually a part of the drama program. Though student shows are sometimes regarded as less important or simply as fun projects (particularly in smaller schools) they do provide other opportunities for trying out, and the auditions context is usually less competitive and threatening. Remember that there are no small parts, only small actors. I have often enjoyed smaller roles because I can sculpt and finish them in more complete detail and with more satisfaction than larger parts. Additionally, student-produced plays are good entrance-level shows for beginning actors. Just as professionals often take advantage of showcase or "freebie" productions to keep in practice or to be seen by producers or agents, students can gain experience in student plays when they are not cast in faculty-directed shows, and their performances will certainly be seen by other directors.

Community theatres

Exposure and experience can be gained not only on campus, but off the campus as well. Although it is always more convenient and, in a certain sense, more protective to perform in college plays, keep yourself open to the possibility of auditioning for and performing in shows done by the surrounding community. If you are cast, civic theatre productions can offer many, many advantages that too often remain untapped by college actors. It is not necessarily true that civic players are always amateurs—housewives with evenings free for leisure time activity, bored businessmen or clerks looking for a social outlet, or high school students helping their parents and teachers put on a local cultural event. On the contrary, many communities have retired professionals doing civic theatre who are wonderful to work with. The American community theatres are now doing fine work in some areas of the country. Indeed, community players, directors, and designers sometimes possess just as much talent and experience as teacher-directors in educational institutions.

The single most important advantage you can gain in community theatre work is the experience of working with people who are likely to treat you as a person, rather than as a college student. When you first audition you will get a taste of what it's like to be an "unknown": you will be up against total strangers competing for roles in a new and totally unfamiliar environment (which may seem far less modern and well-equipped than your college theatre), and you will be judged on the basis of what you can show during the tryouts to directors who know nothing whatsoever about you. This alone is worth the experience of auditioning. You are much more likely to learn your *true* strengths and weaknesses as a performer than you might within a "favored" casting process in your own school by directors who already know you and who may have stereotyped you. In short, breaking away from the campus and testing yourself in civic theatre can give you a foretaste of what the real world of professional auditioning might be like.

This is not to say that community theatre directors will invariably cast or reject you simply on the basis of "objective" merit. No theatre ever works that way. Teacher-directors on university campuses certainly remember what students have done in the past, and they often cast their favorites. Professional directors, too, frequently have their hands tied by producers who want this or that star for a certain role, and they rarely enjoy taking risks with unknown performers for important parts. In civic theatres, you will usually encounter the obstacle of local favorites auditioning for and receiving the choice roles time and again—much like the way in which theatre "groupies" on your campus often have the edge over nonmajors who try out for plays only occasionally. This is sometimes referred to as "paying your dues" (working your way up). You may even have to hang around the theatre as a "tecchie" (technician) for a couple of shows (if you feel the group is worth the effort) before anyone begins to notice you. But once you have successfully carried off a few minor roles or walk-on parts, you will gradually make yourself known to community directors who may then feel more comfortable casting you in roles with more responsibility.

Civic theatres will conduct auditions in much the same way as school theatres. The main thing you should be aware of is what *kind* of civic theatre situation you are getting into. Asking your teachers about the local community stages and the kind of play being done is a good way to start. College and university theatre people are often involved with community work. In fact, many faculty eagerly seek out a place to work with performers with a wider range of experience and ages than can be found on the college campus. In many major cities around the country (San Francisco, Detroit, Los Angeles, Chicago) collegiate faculty have been able to set up experimental theatres which permit them to do more important or difficult work than they could otherwise undertake on campus—theatres which often make a transition from amateur to professional status in a few years.[5]

You can make important contacts for your future performance work by doing community theatre shows. You may also be able to earn money by making yourself available as crew for road shows that occasionally play the community or by becoming eligible for scholarships offered through state community theatre associations. In any case, you are likely to profit from auditioning and acting in shows with experienced community actors, working under different directors, and playing for general audiences who are not thinking of "school drama" when they attend and criticize your performance.

Summer stock and repertory

By far, the most exciting audition and performance experience that you can gain in college is committing your vacation time to working with repertory, dinner, and summer stock theatres. This isn't as formidable as it may sound, and the auditioning challenge is well worth the effort because the learning value of this kind of work is incalculable. For one thing, you can astound yourself by actually getting paid (or at the very least, be "taken care of") while you act—a shot in the arm for your self-confidence.[6] You may also be able to earn college credit through the performing group's academic affiliation with a local school or through internship arrangements with your own school.

Secondly, you will profit from living and working with people who come from different backgrounds and stage experiences. Summer companies run the gamut from "semi-pro" operations, with a handful of lightweight professional actors, to major equity companies, where you can fit in as an apprentice or intern. In both cases you will soak up an immense amount of practical know-how from rubbing shoulders with performers more seasoned than yourself: their techniques, their work habits, and their values.

Auditions for this sort of work are difficult. When you first consider the possibility, be prepared to start at the bottom. No one in the business is going to treat you as a prima donna, no matter how marvelous your successes may have been in college. Many summer groups audition for talent around the country, so competition for the major parts and the best-paying work will be enormous. It is an audition situation rich with challenge.

Don't conclude that someone with relatively little experience hasn't a chance. On the contrary, hundreds of college students are hired each year by summer companies to play major, minor, and walk-on roles required in many shows. And most of these companies do not require that you have professional experience. In fact, many theatres have an arrangement with Actors Equity by means of which nonunion performers can earn their professional status ("Equity card") after a few seasons of summer work. Frequently, too, you will find that young performers are hired as "actor-technicians," which means that they have the chance to perform but will also be expected to work in some technical capacity. Or you may find that the production group has several "companies" for which it is hiring: the major acting company, a children's theatre company, a promotional show company, and so on. So there is a chance that a good audition can pay off. Try to plug into these operations at any level. The benefits of working with a summer company, no matter what the "professional" status or what level you're accepted into, will be available to you.

There are two stages to go through. The first is setting yourself up for the audition. This is the point at which you must begin to take yourself seriously as a professional performer. You will usually be required to submit three things in advance: an application form or letter, a resume, and a photograph. The application is important because you will have to secure references from teachers or directors with whom you've worked, and because it will be used to contact you about when and where the tryouts will be held, plus any additional information regarding the types of audition pieces you are to prepare or the type of show you will be auditioning for. Be sure the application is filled out completely, that your address and/or phone number is accurately and clearly listed, and that the form is returned with accompanying documents *on time*.

Be businesslike and efficient when doing all of this. Recall when you were applying to colleges—choosing which to apply for, getting the paperwork done, keeping a record of who you wrote to and when. Applying for summer theatre work is no different. You need to survey all the groups that are auditioning, note the kinds of plays they're producing, check on the financial and housing arrangements they may offer, note where they are located, estimate how much money you need to live on, see when their seasons run, and so on. Then send your applications to the ones you like.

The second document, the resume, is by far the most important, and more will be said about that in detail in chapter 7. Bear in mind that *the resume is you*. You will have to lay out for producers your experience and abilities, much like a salesman who knows all the products he or she has available. At this point you must step back from yourself and put yourself down on paper as a marketable commodity, as someone an employer would want to hire.

Don't be discouraged if you have little to list on the resume. Avoid feeling like a worm crawling towards the glittering banquet table of the entertainment industry. On the contrary, if you've done any theatre work at all you know that a producing group needs carpenters and scene-shifters and box office assistants and seamstresses fully as much as it needs stars. You will not get paid as much for this kind of work, but you will be needed, and that is what counts. They need people like you, if only for muscle power to shift the scenery. And what you are really going for at this stage of your career is experience, no matter what form it may take. So you do have something to offer. Your photo should be stapled to the back of your resume (more on that later).

This first stage of the auditions process for summer work

is extremely important for you and is one major reason why I strongly recommend summer work for student actors. You will be surprised, once you've assembled the package and made all the arrangements, how clearly you are able to perceive yourself as a potential actor and to present that image to the people who count. Tryouts are often at some distance from your school, so there will be some physical and financial effort required to enter into competition. All of this will help improve your confidence and strengthen your motivation for doing theatre work in your own school.

This is the point at which you will begin to take yourself seriously as a performer. Once you've accomplished the large amount of busywork involved with setting yourself up for tryouts, the world of professional theatre will lose much of its dreaded mystery for you. You will be able to make progress with your work and your ambitions with greater ease.

The second stage of summer auditions involves preparing your audition selections. Just as the salesperson has products or a catalog ready when he or she enters a client's office, so you have your audition pieces ready when you reach the site for tryouts. Other chapters in this book will explain how to choose pieces, get coaching, and work them up. At this point keep in mind that even though you will be launching yourself into that uncertain sea of strange judgmental faces and threatening competitors, you will have your own "arsenal" of selections to rely upon. You'll feel more confident in professional tryouts after twenty or thirty hours of coaching and independent work. So seriously consider summer work after your sophomore or junior year.

The procedures and purposes for summer theatre auditions are different in two respects from those of educational or community theatre. *First, summer theatres are not looking for raw potential. They seek people with entertainment skills. Second, you are auditioning for summer theatres in order to be called back; you are not trying out for a part.* These special considerations will affect many areas of your audition. For example, in choosing your pieces you should avoid any selections which demand quiet, internalized, psychological focus and choose instead those with energy and external vitality. These will give you an edge by showing you to be eager and energetic when producers try to single people out from the crowd. Additionally, a piece with lots of vitality may reveal your ability to project your acting off the stage and into the audience, often made up of vacationers eager for exciting entertainment. Reject Arthur Miller and *Hamlet* and choose instead something by Neil Simon or David Rabe for your general audition.[7]

If summer theatre directors like your general audition, they will call you back and interview you. They may ask you to do something else to see what additional range you have (and that's the place for Arthur Miller or whatever else they might want to see). They'll interview you, and probably they will have you read for a specific part when their company assembles in early summer. "I think the most you can expect from that prepared monologue is a chance to read for a part," observes Cathy Goedert, former casting director at Chicago's St. Nicholas Theatre. "I don't know any actor who's gotten a job from a monologue. So the more you can show me in two minutes of who you are, the more I can get a sort of instinctive feeling about whether I'd like to spend three weeks working intensively with you, whether we're going to 'click.' And the more you can make me laugh, the better chance you've got of coming back to read for a part."[8]

Frequently, you may be performing at combined auditions where the casting people of many summer theatres are watching you. This is a difficult and challenging situation because each group will have different needs, and you won't be able to streamline your pieces for any single theatre. Also, you will usually have only one to four minutes to perform! In this situation you need two vividly staged general audition pieces that develop quickly from the beginning in order to catch the auditors' attention, ones that definitely show that you could probably do more if you are called back. Your two pieces should communicate confidence and stage presence right off the bat, a range of technical skills, and an impression that you are a prepared and disciplined worker. Of course you will also have several other selections prepared so that when you come to callbacks you can "streamline" your presentation.[9] Show the auditors what you can do with zip and with feeling, and you'll greatly increase your shot at a callback.

The entire audition process will give you an exhilarating momentum that you will find extremely satisfying, whether or not you are successful. Don Finn, an acting teacher who auditioned nationally each year for the Hope Summer Repertory Theatre in Michigan, advised his students to plan on a good dinner after tryouts in order to forget all about the nerve-wracking process. When you've gone through the interview, you'll certainly feel like treating yourself to a night out as a well-deserved reward.

final suggestions: Advance preparation and readiness

No matter what auditions situation you may find yourself in, remember that you will never (repeat, NEVER) escape the feeling of stage fright. If you do, then you know that something is definitely wrong. One suggestion about coping with the nervousness of general auditions concerns that indispensable ability of the actor to concentrate. If the general auditions are open, or if you have the opportunity to look over the space and watch others going before you, *study the other performances and the stage carefully.* If nothing else, this activity will help keep your mind off your own rattled nerves. Watch aggressively and critically as others read, mentally commenting upon their readings in a ruthless fashion: what moments seemed to be underplayed or overplayed, what should have been done with the language, where the real meat in the scene is contained, or how you can use the scene to move and stage yourself effectively.

Beg, borrow, and steal line readings, gestures, and reactions that seem right to you. Common sense tells you that watching others (and the director's reactions) is a great way to learn. You get the basic mechanics of the scene straight, you spot what needs to be done with the material, and you avoid performing a cliché. Concentrate on this activity, and resist getting sucked into the "comparisons" trap, the worry trap which can only drain your creative energy and petrify you onstage. *Keep your mind alert.*

While alertness can be practiced during the actual tryouts, you also need to "be prepared" beforehand. This is the single most effective technique which can help you to perform well when your number is called. By this I mean two things: do whatever you can to familiarize yourself with the play in advance, and be physically and mentally in shape to give the performance of your life. Many dramas are readily available as published properties in school and local libraries, and collegiate directors often provide copies of the play that can be signed out in advance of tryouts. Frequently you may also find that the audiovisual department at your school has videotapes or recordings of the show, which is always a better way to learn about a play than reading it.

There is absolutely no excuse for turning up at tryouts unprepared to read from a play that has been announced weeks or even months in advance. And yet I've seen it happen time and again in educational, community, and professional auditions. Student actors are especially lazy in this regard, and I'm frequently appalled by the degree of their ignorance about some of the most famous plays ever written, particularly when copies of the play or recordings are readily available. I invariably place such students at the bottom of my list when it comes to casting because I sense their lack of application. Even if you only have time to read through a play once, your audition will not be entirely cold, and you'll feel much more secure at tryouts.

When you can get the script in advance, don't spend a great deal of time with it. You want to avoid locking yourself into a rigid interpretation of characters or scenes. Let the director do most of that work for you. Instead, try to get a handle on the kind of play it is (wild farce, melodrama, situation comedy), and on the basic events of the plot and the character relationships. Read, watch, or listen to the show with your mind attuned to what parts you might be suitable for (*not* which parts you'd like to play) and what basic things those parts require.

You may find a part that strongly appeals to you, in which case go ahead and choose a short speech to prepare (or even a scene). Directors will sometimes invite auditionees to read a scene of their choice at the end of general tryouts if a student wants to do so and hasn't had the chance. But no director is likely to turn down a prepared scene. Remember also that most directors will not be certain of how a scene should be played. They'll be seeing the play for the first time at tryouts. The interpretation you provide might arrest their attention immediately. If you do single yourself out in this way, your reading should be better than average.[10]

Preparation of yourself

Keep yourself fit and alert by some program of physical exercise. Some students work out regularly by swimming, running, or playing intramural sports (avoid school teams). They can pace themselves as they please and they stay in shape. Laurence Olivier, for instance, used to work out regularly in a gym, feeling that strength and stamina were an actor's most important physical attributes for holding up during a performance. Training in martial arts or Oriental movement meditations such as aikido, yoga, and T'ai-Chi can also be valuable. These keep you fit and train you in centering, concentrating, and breathing. You should always combine these kinds of fitness exercises with performance skills like mime, dance, tumbling, fencing, or gymnastics. Get into the habit of becoming a "compleat actor" early in your college career by developing both your intellectual and your kinesthetic sides. Professional actors (not just starlets) visit the gym regularly.

Ongoing training is especially important for acting students because a performer's body, like his imagination, must be flexible and responsive. He must portray many types of human beings by making his body-instrument as expressive as his voice. You will find that a greater range of skills will be expected of you as your acting matures. Many school directors and summer producers look for people who can act, sing, and dance with some degree of proven skill. As one producer-director in San Francisco remarked: "You really have to be a triple-threat performer to get anywhere these days. Try not to allow your students to get too artsy-fartsy about the kind of acting they do in college or they'll find themselves very limited when they get out and start looking for work."[11] In today's competitive acting marketplace, the well-trained and multitalented actor is no longer the exception but the rule. "Regional theatre producers want actors who can read verse well, who look good and who are physically fit, who can wear a costume, who can play the classics, and who also have emotional resources. . . . Actors nowadays—compared to twenty or thirty years ago—are much better trained. You *expect* someone calling himself an actor to be able to walk properly and speak properly."[12] All of your physical, vocal, imaginative, and intellectual training not only keeps you alert and responsive, but also becomes a bargaining chip in the acting marketplace.

Finally, you should prepare yourself to be mentally in shape for the tryouts. At all costs avoid becoming distracted or overworked when you show up, giving the impression that you just heard about the tryouts a few minutes before or wandered in off the street. Strange as this may sound, I've encountered the situation many times, professionally and educationally. Nothing turns me off faster than a person who drifts lackadaisically onstage—as though it were a Burger King and he or she can't decide what to order. If you take yourself seriously you will be as mentally alert as any professional athlete before the game. To quote actor-director Tom Markus once again: "Your audition is the second most important performance you will give. The opening night performance, or the one that gets reviewed, is the most important. . . . If you give a poor performance at the audition, you'll never have an opportunity to give another."[13]

Getting the self-image straight

Acting is one of the few professions in which professional advancement and success are directly related to one's psychological growth as a human being. As a famous Israeli awareness teacher, Moshe Feldenkrais, has pointed out, "The majority of people in each generation stop growing with sexual maturity, when they are considered to be adult and feel themselves adult. Most learning achieved after that involves essentially what is important socially, and personal evolution and growth are mostly accidental or a fluke. . . . Only artistically inclined people, be they cobblers, musicians, painters, sculptors, actors, dancers, and some scientists continue to grow personally as well as professionally and socially . . . by dint of the art."[14] All of the arts function in this way because every art object—a painting or a player's performance—is in some crucial way an expression of the artist's own sensibilities. A performer "filters" experience—of life, of the play at hand, of the acting ensemble, and the performance environment—by the way he or she sees it. This implies personal values and judgment in selection, emphasis, and communication. Thus your personality is your "sounding board," your artistic "instrument" is yourself—body, mind, emotions. Your "art" can only be as good as your instrument can render it.

When Robert Cohen advises that the "best preparation an actor can make for auditions is to look to his whole development as an actor," he is referring to these awareness skills. You will learn them as your acting matures, and you gain "the confidence, control and authority that come with training and experience."[15] Students don't often think of acting in this "personal" way. Our admiration or excitement about a film or stage performance may disguise itself as exclusively a phenomenon of the writer's skill, the makeup and scenic artists' wizardry, or the technical skills of the actor: voice, body language, spontaneity, or emotional credibility. Or else we may confuse the actor with the characters he or she plays. But if you stop to think about it for a moment you must admit that underneath these features of live performance is something much more fundamental—admiration and appreciation of a human being's ability to so successfully create such a strong illusion or reaction within us.

We are fascinated by that double-natured phenomenon onstage: the performer as a person and as a dramatic character. And this is why you must learn to analyze yourself in order to feel natural and relaxed before the critical eyes of spectators or auditors. You must feel comfortable being vulnerable in performance. Just as you criticize other actors and read them into the roles they play, so too the auditors will read between the lines of your audition in order to learn things about you as a person to work with. And you've got to expect and be ready for this. Self-analysis helps you to know yourself and to understand better what features of your personality might be used to animate the character. Knowing this, you'll reduce your self-consciousness, increase your concentration on acting problems, and make unique choices onstage that will be theatrically compelling.

What this means in terms of an audition is that each time you read for a role you've got to be aware that your first reaction will probably be a defensive one. You'll often seek to present "a character" instead of yourself. This is a common pitfall even for trained professionals, who often attempt to use a character as a mask behind which to hide and disguise themselves. It's important for you to begin early in your career to break down this artificial distinction by realizing that you can play only yourself—those parts of yourself that are suited to the role. It is this *combined* self that the auditors wish to see.

This is never easy to do, but it's absolutely essential for good acting and auditioning. As one professional coach in southern California complains, "The fear that what you feel and express on stage will be taken personally, and yourself held responsible for it, stops most actors. They hide behind the lines and the character, and if it gets hot, they cop out by saying, 'That isn't me. That's the character.' There is only you. There is no character. The character is you."[16] Jane Brody, director of Chicago's Audition Centre, points out that this becomes evident in films. "Those aren't 'characters' you see on the screen. They're people, actors who use and reveal themselves. It's Robert Duvall and Gene Hackman and Al Pacino and not a 'character.' "[17]

If you doubt this, think of President Reagan. The criticism of his background as an actor is based upon this confusion of actor versus character. Of course his personality is one with his screen image. He *is* the same man in the Oval Office as we see in *Bedtime for Bonzo* and other films as well. There is no discrepancy because the characters and the man share identical traits. Charles Marowitz, famous British director and teacher, explains this clearly: "When people denounce a performer for 'playing himself,' what they are really condemning is his basic shallowness and lack of personal resources. . . . The crime is not acting oneself, but not having enough of oneself to act."[18]

Self-discovery exercises

The following exercises are not road maps for achieving personal fulfillment. They'll only introduce you to situations wherein you can and must begin to encounter yourself. They are designed to start you in the direction of forming a clear and strong self-image, a process that will continue during your college career and for many years thereafter. Do them all. As you perform more and more roles and gain experience, you should also be exploring more and more parts of your own personality and thus come to know yourself and your abilities better. These exercises lay the groundwork for self-discovery. The journal entries (Exploration 2) should always reflect your thoughts and conclusions on this growth process.

Exploration 1: Personal analysis

Self-image A—In the left margin of a sheet of paper, write the names of five persons, events, or issues with which you presently have a relationship. These should be key problems or concerns in your life. Each should recur more or less frequently in your everyday thoughts. You should recognize that it is a serious concern that deserves attention. Some possibilities include parents, religion, school, drugs, boyfriend/girlfriend, or career.

Beside each of these concerns, write a single sentence describing how you felt about it three years ago. Then, beside that entry, write another one describing how you feel about it today. Reflect for a bit on the statements you supplied for each of the five items. Try to make them specific, honest, and accurate.

Next, write a paragraph about how you feel your ability

as an actor has been influenced by these changes in your frame of reference. Be certain that you have established a solid connection between acting and the changing frames of reference as you write. Your essay must summarize all of the changes you have noted. It must be a fair and inclusive composite.

Self-image B—Select four people in your life and write a short paragraph for each, describing how that person probably sees you. One should be a parent or family member, the second a close friend, the third a classmate, and the fourth a stranger whom you recently encountered.

Try to write each paragraph as though the words described exactly what that other person saw, felt, or judged about you—almost a quotation or a direct statement by that person. Then, after considering the paragraphs individually, try to combine the ideas into a composite. This should take some time. When you are satisfied your composite is clear and inclusive, write a final paragraph the same length as the others expressing how you feel about yourself. Compare this self-evaluation with the composite.

Self-image C—Divide a sheet of paper into three columns. In the first column write down six words describing yourself that you regard as assets in performance. In the next column, write six words describing what you regard as weaknesses in performance. In order to derive the maximum value from this exercise you should be honest and absolutely ruthless. Try to understand as fully as possible the meaning of each of your key words by calling to mind concrete situations or features that reflect them. Envision the impact of all those traits upon an audience of strangers. This should take some time.

In the final column, write down six tasks or objectives that you honestly feel you can achieve in the next year. These goals should flow from your meditation upon the other key words and may represent physical, emotional, intellectual, or spiritual changes. Try to include with each objective an example of a specific situation by means of which your ideal behavior changes might be identified. This will help to give you some concrete goals to work for.

This exercise can be done frequently: periodically in your journal as a permanent record of personal growth; while rehearsing a role as part of the characterization process; or prior to an audition.

Self-image D—Divide a piece of paper into four columns. Select four screen actors (male or female) whom you enjoy seeing and admire and list them in one column. In the next column, list as many films as you can call to mind in which each actor played. Using the movies as a guide, list in column three the major qualities you admire in each actor. This column should be carefully thought out. Study this column carefully when finished, being certain that each key word accurately describes the specific trait of the performer.

Complete the exercise by identifying in column four at least two ways in which each of the actors has influenced you, physically, emotionally, or intellectually. Or you may choose to identify, on the basis of the acting qualities you noted, the kinds of goals you feel are worth working for and you are likely to reach.

Exploration 2: Journal

Begin as soon as possible to keep a personal journal. It should not be pocket-size (that's a daily notebook, which a student should also have) but fairly large—like a class notebook. Get into the habit of recording impressions at the end of each day: incidents, observations, thoughts, discourses, and so on. Include written exercises contained in this text or material from other theatre classes that you feel to be important. Especially include critical reactions to all performances that you see on film and on stage. Don't feel that you must always criticize major parts; begin instead with the small roles and minor characters.

Criticizing the work of others is a good way to learn, and this should always be done in your acting journal. Self-criticism is also necessary, so be sure that your journal contains or "shares" your important private thoughts as well. Particularly necessary is the discovery of connections between your personal and your "professional" life. When you make an observation or get an insight or "flash," form the habit of "filing it away" for future use.

Remember that you are only beginning to tune your instrument for better sensitivity and that this will be a lifelong process. Whatever you pick up and store away will be used someday, and therefore you should perceive some importance in it for yourself. Ideas often seem common, familiar, and ordinary, but in reality they are not. A good idea is very, very hard to come by, and once it is gone it's lost to you forever. Write down your thoughts, your dreams, the records of your psychic life in addition to your thoughts on acting, the stage, and related subjects.

Journal 1—You have probably heard of the "life studies" that are used in acting training. These are observations and imitations of people, animals, and objects discovered in the student's environment.[19] The great Stanislavski advised life study exercises frequently and urged his pupils to imitate the physical features, speech patterns, even the chain of thoughts ("inner monologues") of people observed and studied on the streets. Get into the habit of really seeing your environment and taking an interest in the people around you, and record your observations. This is fun to do and can lead to minor "adventures" when you find yourself following and eavesdropping on your subjects.[20]

Journal 2—Take an inventory periodically of your physical appearance. Ask yourself what messages you're communicating to others by your clothes, your hairstyle or makeup, your jewelry. What hand and arm gestures do you employ most frequently? Choose a word or two that describes you accurately: your face, physical frame, expression. What areas of your body, external and internal, do you rarely think about? Study your face and eyes closely in a mirror for five to ten minutes, then your full body. Note your observations in terms of what you are expressing to others.

Journal 3—Set aside three or four pages in your journal, pages that you can leave blank for this ongoing project. List in any order the different plays you have been connected with in the past. The list should be exhaustive, that is, it should include *all* play productions no matter how unimportant they may seem to you or how small your part (or crew assignment) may have been. Don't forget to include elementary school plays. Then spend some time thinking about each of those experiences until you can write down beside each entry a single sentence that identifies the most important things you learned from it.

This inventory of your experience and learning should be faithfully kept as you gain more experience onstage. Remember that "learning" includes not only the positive aspects of the activity but the negative ones as well. For example, you may learn what not to do in the future after once becoming involved with a director whom you feel was terrible, or with another actor whose insufferable habits may have caused big problems with the cast or the show. Be sure to consider too some things that may not point directly to a specific performance skill. For instance, it is important to learn how to work with people who might otherwise have nothing in common with you or to discover why an audience may take great enjoyment watching a performance that you may have felt to be rotten or somehow "off."

Journal 4—Begin now to practice "sense memory" exercises for at least one-half hour each day. If you don't know what this exercise consists of, ask one of your teachers. It's simple and basic, but if you practice it faithfully every day you'll be amazed at the number of details stored in your memory and by your ability to re-create situations and experience them vividly in your imagination. This will help you not only in your acting but in your auditioning as well. With an alert imagination, one that can be triggered into action by a few well-chosen images from your sense memory, you can quickly generate belief in the character's environment and become sensorily aware throughout the audition.

Exploration 3: Verbal resume

Prepare a one-minute "verbal resume" about yourself by using as a baseline the questions, "Tell me a little about yourself" or "Tell me what you've done before." Your answer should include and stress the significant items in your theatrical experience: plays you did and whether you acted or ran lights, classes or training and what you learned, and so on. When you've written it all out, commit it to memory so that you can begin practicing it as an actual answer to the director's question. Be sure to confine the package to sixty seconds, comfortably spoken, in a pleasant, "spontaneous," and natural manner. When you're satisfied with the content and the delivery, assemble several friends or your classmates to serve as an audience. Tell them to plug their ears so they absolutely cannot hear you and observe only your body language as you speak.

Tell them to observe and to categorize you as a "type" while they watch and to note what they conclude about the kind of gestures you use, your posture, your energy level, and your facial expressiveness. Collect their observations about what they saw and compare them with the impressions you wished to communicate by your resume.

After you've done this two or three times with your audience, trying each time to bring their impressions of your body language "into sync" with the verbal information, have them unplug their ears and listen to the words. Again gather their comments on how "appropriate" this personal audition seems for you as an individual, using the audience's comments this time to phrase, emphasize, or organize the information more effectively. Your final audience should be your teacher, whose comments should also help you to spot which items of information would be best for special emphasis. Work at this "audition" on an ongoing basis; you may need it at any moment—at a party, at an actual audition session, standing at a bus stop—wherever you might meet someone who's looking for talent and is even only *mildly* curious about your skills. More will be said of this exercise in chapter 7.

Exploration 4: Your self and the character

Look over the monologues by Pavlo Hummel (for males) or by Muffet (for females). It is not important for this exercise that you work up the entire monologue; only the first fifteen seconds are needed. Devise a brief entrance and opening remarks for yourself: walk to the stage, set up a single chair where you want it for the audition, then come downstage and introduce yourself to the auditors. Give them a greeting ("Hello" or "Good morning"), state your name, the character's name, the title of the play, and the playwright's name. Then take a moment or two to "get into the character" and begin the monologue. Your goal in this exercise is to create *two* characters in fifteen seconds: yourself and the dramatic character. You should try to use *every* moment of your entrance and introduction (movement and voice) to establish the first character. Your "attack" on the speech should contrast vividly with the character of your self whom you've just presented. Practice this with friends or classmates until they can "see" two characters emerging in the first fifteen seconds of your audition.

Chapter three

Selecting Audition Material

Always remember that your audition pieces are you. They represent the package you wish to sell the casting people, the fundamental "property" in the transaction. What the auditors conclude about you will be based almost entirely upon the image your material conveys, and your choice of that material reflects how you see yourself. Remember this and think about it; it means that in selecting audition pieces you must be sure that the impression they create of you is one you wish to create and one the director will want to see.

Suitability and appropriateness

The most important criterion of a good audition piece is that it shows you at your best, that it is suitable and appropriate for the kind of person you are. In the previous chapter's explorations you began to take an inventory of your personal and professional traits as a human being. You learned to keep an eye out for the strengths and weaknesses in your acting and began to discover some of their sources as you analyzed your stage experience and personal history. This activity is valuable when choosing material for tryouts because you must be objective about your situation, you must know which aspects of yourself are good to advertise and which are not.

Many young actors make the mistake of selecting pieces that they "like" without regard to whether or not the piece is suited to their abilities and good for the kind of play being cast. Perhaps it was a film or a stage performance that excited them or maybe they studied a play in a drama class during which students and the teacher read some famous speeches and did some good improvs. Or perhaps they were once in a production where another student played the part and turned the audience on. None of these reasons is important (though it's always good to be on familiar speaking terms with dramatic literature). You're not at a tryout to bring another show to life onstage or to show how much you like *Pippin* or *Hamlet*. What's important is whether or not you can handle this piece, and does it give you a chance to show your stuff. If it doesn't reveal your best talents, the director can't possibly know what you can do; and if it's beyond your abilities you'll probably cause embarrassment instead of scoring a favorable impression.

It's impossible of course to find just one or two pieces that display all your abilities, so search out at least a half-dozen to start with. Louis John Dezseran, acting coach at the University of Minnesota, recommends that beginning students establish for themselves "the same standards . . . that you might expect to find in a professional situation. Try using as a model the requirements for the University Resident Theatre Association auditions or the Theatre Communications Group auditions. The U.R.T.A. auditions usually require three short pieces, the T.C.G. auditions two. In both cases, one of these pieces should be from classical literature (drama written before 1800). The total audition should not last more than five minutes."[1] The two or three pieces you perform, though, must be drawn from a repertoire of others. Some actors recommend at least five, others as many as twenty or thirty for the serious working professional. There are two reasons for this: keeping numerous recital pieces on tap permits you to constantly adjust them to your developing abilities and a repertoire permits you to select different pieces for different types of plays being cast.

So, the essential features of a good audition piece are its suitability and appropriateness, both for you as a person and for the play being cast. And there are five tests which you should apply to control this. *First, the selection must conform to your physical type, your vocal range, and your age.* The auditors should be able to "see" you in the role; any audience should be able to believe that at least you "look the part." Avoid pieces in dialect, and stay away from poetic drama when you have no training or skill with verse. And stay within your age range. You'll find this advice contained in many audition books and notices, and you should always follow it.[2] The ages of characters and occasionally their physical and personal idiosyncracies can sometimes be found in the cast list, in stage directions at your character's first entrance, in many of the scene and monologue anthologies listed in the appendix to this handbook, or simply by asking your instructors.

The second test is to be sure your piece is strongly dramatic so that it reveals your best traits. Ask yourself whether or not a potential recital piece has possibilities that are strongly playable. What is "dramatic" in a scene? Well, this can mean many things to different people. However, you should be able to spot in good dramatic material some kind of character development or "discoveries" the character makes, one or more climactic points, a strong and clear conflict (either internal/ psychological or external), and enough turning-points or shifts in direction to permit the character to develop and change with variety and interest. Don't try to knock yourself out and "wow" the director by selecting emotionally explosive materials, however; most of the scenes that might permit you to pull out all the stops come from plays that will have a couple hours of lead-in time before they get to that point. Remain instead within your own emotional and imaginative range. As one director advises, "George in *Our Town* and Nick in *Virginia Woolf* are both boy-next-door types, but the two present as much variety as is needed in a typical audition."[3]

One rule of thumb you must always keep in mind when selecting pieces is that you can never be "better than your material." By this I mean that you can rely upon the work of major, established writers to "sell itself" in a way that a monologue or scene by a lesser-known writer cannot. Your teachers and directors can help you determine the *quality* of potential material; it will "represent" you by reflecting the quality of your judgment in selecting it. In this sense, you are taking personal responsibility for your audition pieces. You want to offer your audience, the auditors, something that is valuable for them to listen to and that will not unduly offend their tastes (such as writing that may include an excessive amount of vulgarity or that needs much sexual suggestiveness in its staging). Letting the material "sell you" as much as possible can definitely give you an edge in tryouts.

The dramatic potential of a scene is usually easier to spot than its potential as a vehicle for your particular talents. This comes from rehearsing and experimenting with the piece. Only when you've analyzed the emotional range of a character, for instance, Helen Keller in *The Miracle Worker* or Father Rivard in *The Runner Stumbles,* and tried to play the selection for awhile will you be able to learn if you can feel comfortable with the portrayal and if you can handle its demands without performing a cliché. Sydney Walker, who teaches auditioning at the American Conservatory Theatre in San Francisco, explains this point in very practical terms for his students: "You have to develop it, structure it, orchestrate it. It must have a beginning, a middle, and an end. Don't, under any circumstances, let the character be at the end . . . where he was at the start. In an audition, honesty and truthfulness just aren't enough. The piece must have strength and variety, and it's got to go somewhere. When you're auditioning, you have only a few minutes to show them what you can do, to reveal that you have a whole spectrum of brilliant colors on your palette and not just one nice little pastel."

The third test of a good audition selection is that it should be out of the ordinary. If you're trying out for a particular play, never choose a scene from that play as your "general audition." You'll be competing against the director's own interpretation of the role. Except in a rare case or two, I've not cast anyone who has done this, because I feel that a student's preconceived ideas of the part—from wherever or whoever the interpretation came—would be too difficult to eliminate or even modify in a short rehearsal period. Select a piece that is similar to the part being cast. Avoid shopworn selections, no matter how famous or powerful or "favorite" they may be. Edmund's "stand up for bastards" speech from *King Lear* or selections from Jules Feiffer's plays are frequently done by inexperienced performers; these selections immediately place them up against famous actors who have done the part or

dozens of other faceless auditionees who have treated the
director to the piece before they came along.

There is also the possibility of adapting material from
nondramatic works—novels, poems, and short stories. Generally speaking, unless you're good at it, you should avoid
this approach because material that isn't written specifically
for actors often lacks the dramatic qualities mentioned earlier.
Narrative prose, for example, is often more discursive than
theatrically exciting, and poetry generally lacks the dramatic
conflict and a focus upon character relationships that a play
selection usually contains.

On the other hand, there is no doubt that such adaptations will be original (I'll never forget the first time I heard a
young professional zing me with Lewis Carroll's *Jabberwocky*,
which was an excellent choice for a children's theatre audition). From studying one-person shows like those of Hal Hol-
brook or Julie Harris *(The Belle of Amherst)*, you can learn much
about adapting materials for tryouts. A class in oral interpretation or reader's theatre is excellent training for this.

No agreed-upon rule exists concerning adaptations for a
tryout piece. One director will recommend that you stick to
theatrical selections so at least the fundamental dramatic requirements will be met. Other directors (myself included) will
often perk up when a student presents something original,
because it suggests he or she is intelligent and creative. Still
others will recommend something totally off-the-wall, either
to score an unforgettable impression or to simply have on
hand when the occasion warrants. Remember that no one can
actually pick pieces for you (and never let anyone do so)—
they may only recommend. You are the one who must decide
and then live with your selections; you must feel confident
that they are the best ones to represent you.

*The fourth criterion for choosing selections is that the total pack-
age is tidy and that it covers the range of your talents.* By "tidiness"
I mean the sense of purpose you display when you get onstage. As a director I want to see people act when they audition, and they should be keenly aware that they have only
a few minutes in which to do it. My time is too valuable (and
I will assume that their time is valuable too) to waste it in
listening to where the monologue occurs in the play, what

motivates the character, what the plot of the play might be, or how the imaginary setting is supposed to look. Director Bill Oliver of San Francisco's One-Act Theatre Company calls this sort of thing the "kiss of death" for an auditionee. I expect an auditionee to "take stage" when he or she is called: to command or "own" that unfamiliar space, to ignore distractions, to be "present" or focused when I look up and give my attention.

Remember that the way you introduce yourself speaks eloquently about you. Get your furniture set up right away. Your opening remarks should be pleasant and direct: your pieces should require no more introduction than the name of the character and the title of the play. Any other essential background should be given in a single sentence: "Her sister is seated downstage with a knife in her back, listening." Never pick a scene to do alone in which more than one character is involved unless you have edited out the other character's lines. An imaginary character onstage, however, is always a good rule of thumb: it gives you someone to play to, a "vis-a-vis" to play off and some physical point to connect with. Do not pick a scene with crucial props or furniture—avoid cluttering the space and boring the auditors with a dull explanation. *Pick material that requires only that you act.*

Your method of exiting is another demonstration of your seriousness or the lack of it. Be brisk and businesslike: thank the auditors for their time and don't excuse yourself or mumble or shuffle off self-consciously. Your audition package should have a brief introduction, two or three prepared pieces, and a simple "thank you" at the end to cap it all. If the director wants to know more about you or your skills, he or she will ask.[4]

Your abilities and potential as a performer are also expressed by the way in which your pieces "say it all" about you, the way they connect and relate. This comes out principally in contrasting features—comic and serious, light and heavy, ballad and "belt." Be certain that these contrasts are sharp—that a certain emotional quality, a certain mood, a particular character trait in one piece is not also found in the next piece. You waste time at an audition by repeating yourself. Above all remember that "versatility" and "variety of talent" mean simply covering your range. If you haven't got much of a range, don't pretend that you have. Do only what you can do well, what you can perform with honesty and authenticity, and no more.

The fifth and final criterion of a good audition piece is that it be "original." It is impossible to define exactly what directors mean by this, but in general it refers to the personal stamp that you alone can place upon the reading. Following the preceding third criterion or test and rejecting overworked pieces certainly has much to do with originality. And touching base on the fourth test of versatility will ensure that the director sees those qualities which you feel you can do especially well. But your audition pieces become original only when you've poured yourself into them, taken a hand from start to finish in shaping them for someone else's appraisal. You will communicate your skills by means of your selection just as you will by your presentation.

The surest guideline for achieving originality is the degree to which you can identify with your character's situation, his or her mood in the scene, the depth and the sensitivity of feeling, and the character's reactions to the circumstances. In part, of course, this is an actor's gut feeling—something that the player has always been expected to do—but it also depends upon the actor's understanding of his or her own feelings, thoughts, and emotions, and willingness (or unwillingness) to own them. Pick a piece that ultimately turns you on because that speech has got to be your friend through thick and thin. To quote Sydney Walker again, "Choose audition material that you love, so that the belief is already there, and you don't have to whip yourself into a frenzy to sell yourself on material you don't really believe in. This is one of the few instances where the actor is in the driver's seat in terms of choosing material, and it should be meaningful to him."[5]

A character's life is only partially sketched in by the playwright, who knows that the remainder—the center, the key element of characterization—must come from the actor's own personality. This is just as true of finished performances as it is of auditions: the director *wants* to be touched, affected, somehow moved by a good, believable reading, wants to watch your ability in bringing a character to life up there, and not just performing a list of character traits. Learn to give yourself over to your character's feelings in the scene—all of them. Learn to enter into the character's attitude and own it.

In all of your acting you must learn to project your *self*, and use your self in this way to enter the world of your character. In auditions you have only a few minutes in which to live in that world and believe in it. After listening to dozens of auditions and seeing people "acting" like crazy, the bored casting director is always attentive to someone who is unafraid to reveal this special "germ" of a character by authentic emotion, by economy and honesty, and by simple reactions to the dramatic situation at hand.[6]

Regard your audition selections as blueprints that you must follow but that need the personal skills of a master builder (actor) in order to bring them to life, to explore and exploit the scene for its full potential. Use others' opinions to test for these qualities in your piece; invite criticism from your acting class or even from your roommates. Do some personal evaluation with videotape if you can. The best feedback, of course, will come from a good coach, but more on that in chapter 4.

Be certain your audition pieces represent you, that you can honestly identify with those characters in order to bring them to life. In all historical periods this has been the most fundamental requirement of the player: to project one's own life, belief, and commitment into the role. By becoming aware of your own traits as a person, by following the self-image exercises—and others like them—in the preceding chapter, you'll grow to feel more comfortable revealing yourself in public. As one professional actor commented to my workshop group, "You have to really want to do it. It just means more to you than most things in life, being up there onstage."[7] Remember that without belief in what you're doing, the other four qualities I've been discussing will never add up to a good audition.

Where to locate material

Your drama department has posted a notice of tryouts for a Shakespearean play, announcing that students should bring something to present to the auditors.[8] A community stage group has placed a casting notice in the local newspaper, announcing tryouts for a Neil Simon Broadway comedy. In late winter you see your school's bulletin board covered with notices of summer theatres auditioning for musical comedies. Where do you begin to look for material?

Common sense tells you right off the bat that you're liable to be a dead duck if you've waited until the last moment to think of "something you can do." It always irks me when students come to me a month before the U.R.T.A.s or summer stock auditions and ask, "Can you help me find something to use?" I do it, of course—even a last minute shot is better than none at all, and the audition experience in itself is valuable. But as a general rule, these students never have much success in serious competitive situations, especially where bucks are involved, and unless they are extremely talented, I never recommend them for serious auditions like U.R.T.A. You should take yourself more seriously and be ready (even eager) to perform. Your rewards will be directly proportionate to the degree of your application.

The very best way to discover material for auditioning is to read. If you're serious about your studies you should try to read at least two plays each week, and by attending plays and watching films you can expose yourself to even more. Obtain recordings of plays and musical theatre sound tracks from your school or community libraries, your teachers, or your friends. Survey courses in theatre, English, or comparative literature are also valuable (in addition to those that are required) because you'll investigate the historical-cultural context and learn about manners, conventions, and style. Independent studies projects under a tutorial by a good professor are also helpful. Break away from TV viewing and sink your teeth into something real; learn to utilize your spare time productively (a paperback play is easy to slip into your pocket or purse for idle moments or long rehearsals). Ingest all you can while in college because you'll never find as much spare time and encouragement to learn and read once you get out into the real world.

With this kind of informed background, you can then turn to the student's primary source for auditions material: anthologies of scenes and monologues specially prepared for this purpose. Generally these fall into two categories: "classical" selections or "famous scenes" and contemporary scenes/monologues. These anthologies may already be part of your program of study because they are frequently used in acting classes. There are many on the market. Teachers are constantly demanding fresh material from editors and publishers. The Appendix lists a half-dozen of these collections currently in print, and your instructors can probably recommend others. In addition to providing you with ready-made cuttings of plays, these books also give you synopses of the entire play, character background, acting problems to explore with the piece, and other helpful hints. They are suitable for working alone, with a partner, or with a coach. They are available only in paperback, so buy them—you'll be using them a long time.

A second way of locating material is to find it in recordings, films, videotapes, and television broadcasts of theatre programming. Plays that are presented on the electronic media are, of course, readily available in book form; and scenarios of famous films can occasionally be found too, especially as film and media studies become more widespread as subjects in the academic curriculum. Finally, attending plays frequently is a very good way to spot speeches or scenes that are potentially of value to you.

There are two things to be careful about here. One problem you'll have to solve is correcting the passive way in which we usually listen to stereo or watch TV and films. Develop the skill of listening carefully and watching critically. Mentally comment to yourself upon the presentation in order to keep alert and to avoid the "narcosis" that often sets in. Follow the recording in a playscript if you can. Turn off the TV commercials and even the audio on the TV in order to concentrate instead upon body language, staging, and rhythm. This is one "price you must pay" for being a theatre student—being more than just the average consumer-spectator. Never just sit back and let it all wash over you; your acting/directing/criticizing mind should always be at work.

The second mistake to avoid with media presentations is forming a fixed interpretation of how to play a part. Remember that acting style is always "reduced" for the camera: gestures are more restrained, vocal qualities are more "homogenized" by the sound track, blocking patterns are usually less extreme and noticeable, and emotional peaks are more controlled. You will have to modify your presentation in several important respects. You wouldn't want to copy another performance anyway, so be sure that you take a free hand with material like this when you first rehearse it. Play it to extremes, magnify it in order to break down any imitative tendencies you may have formed and to explore/exploit the selection as far as it will permit.

A final source of audition material is suggestions by others: your teachers, other actors, and attending and observing tryouts frequently. You will be surprised how many suggestions for good material can occur when you just listen for them. Your head can be like a spy's radio set, which, when tuned to a given channel, picks up the proper station when it happens to broadcast. How many times when attending a film or a play have you heard someone (or yourself mentally) comment upon the performance by saying "That was a great scene" or "I like the way she did that" or "Do you remember the part where . . .?" This kind of immediate gut reaction often zeros in on good dramatic material that you might be able to use. Get used to listening to others' casual comments and to your own reactions with audition possibilities in mind.

Your teachers, of course, will be a major source of suggestions. First of all, they may be recommending things to you indirectly. Look back over the roles you've played and the shows you've done, bearing in mind the possibility that your director may have staged a speech or a scene in such a way that a good, solid, dramatic moment was achieved. If so, was it early or late in the play, would it need a few hundred lines for the character to work up to the required level, or does it develop and build pretty much by itself? If it was a scene, could you edit out the other characters and their lines (if any) and play it to an imaginary listener by simply joining your character's remarks together? You can also do this to plays and poems that you studied in class. Do you recall characters or moments that read well or that were discussed as important? Did you study poetry by reading it aloud to yourself several times (as you always should do)? Which poems were fun to explore in this way? Generating your own ideas in this manner before approaching someone else for suggestions will automatically guarantee that any material that you eventually use will be easier to enter into and identify with.

When asking your teachers for audition pieces remember that only you can make the decision whether to use them. They know what might be good for you, but only you can know if it feels right. Read your coach's suggestions aloud several times slowly and carefully before doing anything; just sit there and let your imagination react to the lines and suggest ideas. Then move at random through the space while reading. Allow your movements to respond to the text: give in to changes in the tempo, to inclinations for gesturing, turning, crossing, sitting, etc. Before you take them back to your coach work them experimentally like this, feeling them out instead of definitely setting anything. Your coach will then see a few more things to do with them, or he may decide a couple are unsuitable. You too will find your initial impressions changing after this first run. But whatever decisions you or your coach may reach, exploring your pieces tentatively at first will be valuable: you will find it easier either to scrap an inappropriate selection or to build upon a good one if you've already worked out the basic interpretation.

Remember that it is always hard to distinguish between a piece which really feels right for you and one that feels right only because a coach whom you respect has recommended it. Most of the time you will listen to your instructors because you feel they know what they're lecturing about, and you follow your director's instructions because that's the way things are done in theatre. It's a dictatorial operation in many respects because it has to be. Other actors, too, may recommend suggestions to you. But when it comes to picking your pieces (and later staging them) you are the best judge of what is good for you to perform and what is not. After all, it will be you alone—not your instructor or your friends—who will be up there selling your abilities for the part or the summer job. So consider carefully all suggestions with the idea of "selling yourself" in mind. When it comes to performing an audition piece, you want to be able to "stand behind your product." Katinka Matson, a Southern California actress and casting agent, states this in no uncertain terms in her book on the profession: "In all your preparation and training, you are ultimately responsible for yourself. No one else can *make* you do anything, no matter how inspiring he may be. . . . Remember that you are your own product, advertising agency, and salesman, and that no one but yourself can attract the attention of your audience and keep it fascinated."⁹

Exploration 5: Editing-Out

Study the following scene from George M. Cohan's *Seven Keys to Baldpate* and the audition speech which was edited from the scene. Notice how the other character's lines have been eliminated, and patches have been added to bridge the gaps. Notice also how the new piece retains the character's constantly changing thought pattern while building uninterruptedly to a climax—which of course must be played in extreme melodramatic style and with absolute belief for proper effect.

Original Scene

Myra:	(*Up close to him*) Will you please tell me your name?
Magee:	Well, a name doesn't mean so much, so you may call me Mr. Jones. And yours?
Myra:	My name is—(*Hesitates. Mary and Mrs. Rhodes lean over balcony, listening.*) Listen! (*Brings Magee downstage.*) My husband is the president of the Asquewan-Reuton Suburban Railway Company. He has agreed to pay a vast amount of money for a certain city franchise; a franchise that the political crowd at Reuton has no power to grant. They are going to cheat him out of this money and use it for campaign funds to fight the opposition party at the next election. If he sues for his money back, they are going to expose him for entering into an agreement he knows to be nothing short of bribery. The present mayor is at the bottom of it all.

Seven Keys to Baldpate, by George M. Cohan. Reprinted by permission of American Play Company, Inc.

(*Mary and Mrs. Rhodes start at mention of mayor's name.*) I ran to my husband tonight and begged him not to enter into this deal. I warned him that he was being cheated. He wouldn't believe me, but I know it's true. He's being cheated, and will be charged with bribery besides. That's why I risked the mountain on a night like this. I must have been followed, for I was shot at as I reached the top of Baldpate. Oh, I don't know who you are, but you're a man and you can help me. (*Puts her hands on his shoulders, pleadingly.*) You will help me, won't you?

Magee: (*Interested*) Yes. What do you want me to do?

Myra: (*Looks at Magee for a moment without speaking, then goes up to a safe and back to Magee*) In that safe there is a package containing two hundred thousand dollars.

Magee: (*Goes up toward safe*) Two hundred thousand dollars! (*Mary and Mrs. Rhodes start downstairs very slowly.*)

Myra: (*Following Magee up R.*) That's the amount. It must be there. A man named Bland was to bring it here and deposit it at midnight. Cargan was to follow later, and was to find it here.

Magee: (*Coming down stage*) Cargan coming here!

Myra: So they've planned it. I must have that money out of there before he arrives. You'll help me, won't you? Don't you understand? My husband is being cheated, tricked, robbed, probably ruined.

Magee: But I don't know that combination.

Myra: (*Wringing her hands*) Oh, there must be something we can do! Please, please—(*She kneels at his feet and puts up her hand imploringly.*) For the sake of my children, help me, please![10]

Audition Piece Edited from Original Scene

Myra: My name is—Listen! (*She listens but hears nothing. Continues:*) My husband is the president of the Asquewan-Reuton Suburban Railway Company. He has agreed to pay a vast amount of money for a certain city franchise, a franchise that the political crowd at Reuton has no power to grant. They are going to cheat him out of this money and use it for campaign funds to fight the opposition party at the next election. If he sues for his money back, they are going to expose him for entering into an agreement he knows to be nothing short of bribery. The present mayor is at the bottom of it all. I ran to my husband tonight and begged him not to enter into this deal. I warned him that he was being cheated. He wouldn't believe me, but I know it's true. He's being cheated, and will be charged with bribery besides. That's why I risked the mountain on a night like this. I must have been followed for I was shot at as I reached the top of Baldpate. Oh, I don't know who you are, but you're a man and you can help me. You will help me, won't you? In that safe there is a package containing two hundred thousand dollars. It must be there. A man named Bland was to bring it here and deposit it at midnight. Cargan was to follow later, and was to find it here. I must have that money out of there before he arrives. You'll help me, won't you? Don't you understand? My husband is being cheated, tricked, robbed, probably ruined.

Now turn to the Appendix and make your own adaptations for monologues drawn from two-character scenes. Begin with the character of George in Bernard Slade's comedy *Same Time, Next Year*. Try to retain the storytelling quality of the original scene, leaving time to feel through each image as fully as possible. Try also to retain George's sense of self-mockery as he tries to project his own foolishness upon his wife. Repeat this exercise with the character of Judith in Albert Innaurato's serio-comic scene from *Gemini*. Be sure to retain the nervous fragmented delivery pattern as she desperately and awkwardly tries to deal with Francis's homosexual problem. Allow her two or three moments to "touch bottom" with some authentic, articulate gut feelings.

Exploration 6: Condensing a selection

Take the following speeches and edit them down to no more than two minutes' playing time. The speech by the bloodthirsty psychotic Saint-Just, given before the National Assembly, has been taken from Büchner's *Danton's Death*. It capitalizes upon a slow but steady build to a powerful climax. Retain opportunities for as much vocal dynamics as possible: changes in pitch, stress, and tempo; rapidly alternating moods and inflections; and phrasing that needs skills in articulation and projection.

Saint-Just, from *Danton's Death*

There seem to be some people in this assembly who have remarkably sensitive ears. They can't bear the mention of the word "blood." I think a few general observations should be enough to convince you that we are no more cruel in our methods than Nature or, for that matter, Time. Nature proceeds in accordance with her own laws, quietly and irresistibly and when Man comes into conflict with her, he loses, he is annihilated. A very slight change in the chemistry of the air, a flare up of volcanic fire, or a shift in the equilibrium of a mass of water, an epidemic, or an eruption, or a flood is all that's needed to cause the death of thousands. And what is the result? Seen in perspective, it is a meaningless, almost imperceptible change in the physical disposition of Nature. A change which would pass unnoticed, if it did not leave a few corpses in its wake. I ask you whether the moral universe in her revolutions ought to be more considerate than the physical universe? I ask you, should not an idea have as much right as a law of Nature to destroy the things that stand in its way? Can anyone, in fact, imagine that an experience which has changed the whole nature of mankind, and of the world, should stop short of spilling a little blood? The forces that rule the universe make use of us in the world of the spirit just as certainly as they make use of floods and volcanoes in the world of Nature. What difference can it make if men die of an epidemic or a revolution? Mankind advances so slowly, its steps are counted in centuries, and beneath each step we find the graves of whole generations. The most simple discoveries and the most basic truths cost millions of lives! So, isn't it obvious that now, at a time when history has been gathering speed, more people should find themselves out of breath? Our conclusion, therefore, is this: We were all born equal, except for those differences which Nature herself determined; what merits we have belong to all; but privilege belongs to no one, not to

Danton's Death, translated by William Oliver. Used by permission of William Oliver.

an individual, not a class, great or small. Now, each and every practical application of this argument has cost its lives, stage by stage. July fourteenth, August the tenth, May the thirty-first, remember! These are its punctuation marks! It took just four years, four years! Under normal circumstances, it would have taken a whole century to achieve this, a whole century punctuated, of course, with generations. Is it so astounding, then, that the flood of revolution should need to cast up its dead bodies at every bend and halt? We still have propositions and amendments yet to be tried! Are we to be hindered in this by a few hundred corpses? Moses led his people through the Red Sea and into the wilderness, until the old corrupt generation had been annihilated, and then, only then, he founded his new state. Citizens and legislators! We have neither the Red Sea nor the wilderness at our disposal, but we do have war and we have got the guillotine! The Revolution is like the daughter of Pelias: she dismembers mankind so that it shall be rejuvenated. The human race is going to rise from the cauldron of blood, as the earth did once from the waters of sin, rise with renewed strength in its limbs, as strong as if it were created new. We invite all secret enemies of tyranny, wherever they may be, in Europe or anywhere on the face of the earth, all men that carry Brutus' hidden dagger, we ask them to join us now, and share this exalted moment![11]

The following speech by the young waitress in William Hauptman's *Comanche Cafe* should contain as many of the original selection's rich variety of images as possible. Connect them so the actress can imaginatively identify with the character's fantasies and can play them fully, enthusiastically. Try to set up sharply contrasting moods and imaginary scenes as you edit in order to capture the character's desperate yearning for exotic and exciting locales and her quickly changing goals as she speaks in a dream world of her own.

Ronnie, from *Comanche Cafe*

There's a whole mysterious country out there, Mattie, and I'm going to see it all. As soon as I can, I'm leaving. I'm going to see Chicago and New York—the big cities up North where everybody stays up all night long drinking black coffee. Life's more serious up there. I've heard those all-night programs where people phone in and talk about their problems. They've got a lot of serious problems up there, that's all I've got to say. I want to see Grand Central Station, the crossroads of America, and the tallest buildings in the world. Skywriting floating on the clouds above the buildings all day long. See Tin Pan Alley and Times Square and newsboys everywhere you look and gangsters and baseball players. People talk in newspaper headlines. Every place is going out of business and everybody can be bought. Or I might go to California, where the sun's always hot and you can see the movie stars walk into the drugstore and buy aspirin just like normal people. I might go there—I might—there's orange groves and private eyes, and they say it never rains. Or I might go down South, where people burn crosses on the lawns and hide their idiot sons in the attic. To Florida, where hotels look like big white wedding cakes, and millionaires drive down the boulevards with the top down, smoking cigars. Moonlight and palm trees and waterspouts! Things I never saw before! Or I might even go to Georgia, where nobody ever goes. To the mountains, where it's always raining cats and dogs, and the hillbillies play their fiddles and drink moonshine. They marry down there when they're eleven years old. You don't know what you might do down there! The rain pours down, and there's a house I heard about where there's no more law of gravity and water runs uphill. Wonderful things! Wonderful things all over America! And I'm going to see them all. Just let me go anyplace but here—in Oklahoma.[12]

Chapter four

Preparing Audition Pieces

At every stage of the rehearsal process you must learn to work alone. If you constantly expect your teachers or your coach to tell you what to do with your audition piece, you really have no business doing it at all. Only by committing a lot of your own time to an audition project can you expect your scenes or monologues to reflect the best of your abilities and to project confidence and purposefulness when they're presented. The interpretation must be your own, the blocking and business should be self-devised, the vocal dynamics must feel familiar and comfortable to you, otherwise you'll come across like a robot performing someone else's mechanical instructions. Discipline and commit yourself seriously to a systematic method of preparation for monologues, just as your director expects you to memorize lines and polish your acting outside of play rehearsals. Remember that acting is work and that it usually pays off for people who are serious about it.

Getting your act together

The approach laid out in this chapter covers all the necessary bases for preparing your audition pieces by yourself and then working with a coach. The specific exercises, however, are only general methods that are commonly employed in many acting studios and collegiate drama departments. They assume that you've already had some class work in acting fundamentals because no handbook of this sort can teach you how to act. So treat these exercises as reminders, summaries of techniques you've already learned, or brush-up methods.

Whether or not every exercise will work for you is unimportant; each actor develops techniques over the years that work best for him or her and which may or may not be useful for someone else. I've found these approaches to be fairly standard in my classes and workshops—they seem to offer something to most of the undergraduates I work with. Try each exercise at least once to see if it can help you. In no case omit any of the fundamental steps in the overall approach: paraphrasing, goals and obstacles, beats, and so on.

Finally, a word about language. In speaking with theatre people across the country while gathering material for this handbook, the single most important comment I heard from all quarters was the need for auditionees to understand and to fully play each and every word in their monologue. There is absolutely no substitute for literary analysis; an actor must be intelligent and sensitive to what he or she is saying.

As an acting student you should be aware that our society has conditioned you to use an extremely narrow range of your vocal and verbal resources. The influence of TV and film has been immense because of their electronically controlled audio tracks, their hypervisual emphases, and their pedestrian hack-writing. All of us are induced to speak in half-sentences or one-line clichés, and to rely upon language that is no more complicated than that used to order lunch at a fast food diner. People don't come to the theatre to hear this sort of drivel— they turn on their tube for free when they want "brain candy" for escape and diversion. As a stage actor, though, you'll be expected to handle a range of speech patterns drawn from characters of every historical and cultural period and with enormously complicated psychological drives.

Don't fall into the trap of assuming that only academics and students engage in literary analysis or that Shakespearean and Edwardian dialogue can be approached in the same way as Neil Simon's witty and articulate conversations. Many people in professional theatre have pointed out to me the value to an actor of a liberal arts background in English, psychology, and history. If you can diagram sentences, then do so until you understand the syntactical sense of your monologue—its complicated arrangement of principal and subordinate clauses, modifiers, parenthetical remarks, and the rest. Just as the previous chapter urged you to get into the habit of constant reading, the first part of this chapter encourages you to master some tools of literary analysis that will help you. As one actor-director remarked to me, "After all, you've only got yourself and the word up there at an audition. You've got to tear that monologue apart word for word and make friends with each and every idea, identify with the images and the emotions—what Stanislavski called the 'diction,'— fall in love with those words and make sense of them."[1]

Working on your own

Your first step in working up an audition piece is to prepare three copies of the monologue or scene. This should be the final version of your piece after you've trimmed the original to an appropriate length and edited out the lines, characters, and stage directions you don't need. Type your material double spaced. Scenes should also be typed even though they're longer. Sometimes scenes are published in a format that leaves enough space for writing in the margins and between the lines. Two of the copies will be used as working drafts, the third should be set aside for your final version. When working on these copies, always use a pencil.

Paraphrase

The second step in preparation is to paraphrase the selection. A paraphrase is a restatement of the character's language and feelings in your own words (it should always turn out to be longer than the original). Be sure that you understand the surface or literal meaning of each word and image, as well as the underlying or subtextual meanings that the words convey. These are commonly called the denotative and connotative meanings; both are important to think about, and both are important to paraphrase.

On the literal level, there are many words and idioms in classical plays that only a dictionary or a professor can explain to you, and modern plays contain slang, regional, jargon, or ethnic terms that you must understand before you can make sense of the piece and learn about your character. Don't assume you understand material simply by reading it over a couple of times. Spend time with it and think it out, making certain you know exactly what's being said. You'd be surprised how even experienced actors fail to do this with audition material and with finished performances in productions.

The connotative meaning is less easy to identify from a dictionary, although you'll find in the entry all the subordinate meanings of a word and these can be helpful. There are special dictionaries for certain language areas, such as the *Dictionary of Slang* and similar reference books. As we saw in chapter 2, book work is an important tool for play and character analysis. Any clues you can dig up about your character will be grist for your mill.

But word meanings are only partial clues. You'll find the subtext of your monologue or scene will emerge more clearly as you rehearse and begin to sense what underlies the character's spoken words. These underlying meanings are hidden emotional dynamite in plays, because they energize the spoken text. Do you call your boyfriend a "neat guy" or "a hunk" or "my man"? They all mean the same but their implications are different (both for you and for him), and their impact upon listeners will be different in each case.

Connotative meanings are especially revealing. They add much wider applications to a character's words—more "levels of meaning" to the spoken text. The subtext can be either in agreement with or in opposition to it, but it is always more complex and closer in touch with the character's true emotional needs. To put it another way, recognize that language is only a partial clue to what the character really wants or intends to communicate.

Learn to tap this subtext and to read between the lines of a scene. Ask yourself what the character really meant by a word, phrase, or remark. The more questions an actor can ask, the more creative and insightful his performance will become. Was your character forced to phrase words carefully? To whom is he or she speaking? What is the real issue at stake in the scene or monologue? How might the environment or situation be influencing what the character says?

You may be able only to identify part of the connotations that words and phrases contain when you do your initial paraphrase, but it's important to speculate on the subtext because in cold readings you'll have very little time to discover and to play it. Begin with prepared readings: tear your material apart and start asking questions. You'll find the answers will come easier as you go along.

To conclude, your denotative paraphrase must reveal all the surface meanings of the character's words; this is the "strategy"—the outward means your character employs to express inner needs. Your connotative or subtextual paraphrase must reveal the character's deepest, strongest motivations; it must give you vivid suggestions for concrete actions—what to do, how to move and actually play the scene. When you're in command of the subtext you'll be able to fill the spoken words with energy and drive, using them to create a striking, vivid performance.

Exploration 7: Paraphrasing

Study the speeches by the Duchess and George in the Appendix and the sample paraphrases following each. Remember that these paraphrases are done in the words of one student actor and that yours would be phrased differently because your language style and personal associations are unique. The literal rewording of the Duchess's speech tries to capture the ideas of a young woman who is a very good looking, wealthy, and attractive widow, while the connotative rewording shows the emotional sources of the spoken text. The denotative paraphrase of George's speeches (patched together to form a single speech) tries to retain an important note of rationalization; hindsight covers up or glosses over the character's embarrassment, while the subtextual paraphrase brings this embarrassment and the character's comical need to blame someone else fully into focus. In each case the denotation solves any difficult problems with meaning and helps you to personalize the speech by putting it into your own words. The connotation taps these characters' gut reactions and basic needs, thus giving you a driving force for *acting* the words.

Now look over the speech by Johnny in Charles Gordone's *No Place to Be Somebody* and the speech by Pavlo from *The Basic Training of Pavlo Hummel*. Paraphrasing the literal meaning contained in the black dialect should provide challenging research opportunities for you. Read or listen to the entire plays in order to write up paraphrases of the subtext in each selection. By uncovering the sources of Johnny's images you'll discover the ironic mockery that the angry outburst contains. These qualities are very playable; they suggest points of vocal emphasis, for example, like how to pace and time the delivery, where the articulation of words and sounds can be helpful, and how to control volume.

When you've completed these projects turn to the more difficult selection by Puck from Shakespeare's *Midsummer Night's Dream*. For the literal meaning you'll need to visit the library and use a "variorum" edition of the play: a script that contains a glossary of word meanings and line interpretations. You should also read the entire play (if you haven't already) in order to understand the context. This is very important. Once you've completed your own denotative and connotative paraphrases, compare your restatement against the original in order to appreciate some of the advantages of using verse language instead of prose. Have your coach or theatre professor help you with this step. Ignore the obvious difference of "old fashioned" language and unusual syntax. Focus instead upon such things as economy of words, the rhythmic sound of the lines, or the phrasing. What does the poetic form enable you, as an actor, to achieve that everyday prose language does not?

The next step is to practice these three speeches aloud, trying to keep only the literal meanings clearly in mind as you speak. Avoid the temptation to rush and to run together words and phrases—especially in the Shakespearean selection. Don't pantomime anything except in the most difficult passages. Taste the images in your mind *before* they enter your mouth. Try to deliver the speech with as much clarity of expression as possible and to motivate your delivery so it seems natural. When you feel you're ready, test yourself by having someone listen to you. Ask that person how much of the speech was understandable the first time through (75 percent is a good average). Also ask how much of the speech was believable.

The final step is to deliver the monologue while stressing only the connotative meanings and asking your listener how the literal sense of the speech seemed to change. This is by far the most difficult part of the exercise. You might begin by whispering the subtext several times before gradually moving into a whispered delivery of the spoken text. Gradually increase your volume until you can speak in a full voice without losing complete touch with the subtext. You can practice this part alone by using a tape recorder. Record the connotative paraphrase with great intensity, and allow it to play underneath your delivery of the actual text in the practice session. Most important of all, give in to all impulses for extreme movements and gestures and for radical vocal delivery patterns that the emotional subtext suggests.

Goals, obstacles, and actions

The third step in preparation is to identify the goals and obstacles of your character and choose concrete actions that express them. Identifying and then playing objectives and obstacles are the hardest things to master in acting and auditioning, but this skill lies at the heart of a good performance. Liv Ullmann, the Swedish actress noted for her work with Ingmar Bergman, has remarked that "everything we portray onstage ought to be shown from two sides. When I smile I must also show the grimace behind it. Try to depict the countermovement—the counter-emotion. . . . Only then, when no situation or character is obviously good or evil, is it truly significant to act."[2] Michael Schulman, one of New York's most respected acting teachers, points out that goals and obstacles "and the uncertainty they generate with regard to outcomes . . . constitute the basic structure of a dramatic event."[3] Train yourself to spot what your character is struggling for (goal, intention, objective) and what prevents him or her from attaining it (the obstacles). Then you'll find it easier to devise concrete actions to play onstage moment by moment that will express those intentions clearly.

To begin with, you should realize that a character's objectives in a scene can be either single or multiple and that you have to be as specific as possible in pinning them down. Your character will most likely shift objectives in a scene as it develops and he or she learns something new, encounters different obstacles, responds to other characters, or decides upon a new goal to pursue. Monologues will usually have one main objective—the character's overall intention behind the speech—that must be broken down into a series of minor objectives that lead the character through the speech. Once you've settled upon these objectives keep working at them until you reduce them to clear, one-syllable nouns and verbs.

The next step is to devise a chain of specific actions you can play onstage that express the character's intention and that add up to fulfilling the character's objectives. Occasionally one or more actions might be found in the stage directions: the way a character speaks, gestures, or moves onstage may be suggested by the playwright. Here again, though, you need to scrutinize these and decide whether something more vivid would work better. Most frequently you'll find nothing indicated in the script. Remember that stage directions are almost always taken from the stage manager's promptbook of the original production, and what served well in a play production may be less vivid than what you need (or feel you would like to do) with the same piece in an audition.

One repertory theatre director of wide experience, William Glover, stated this idea in practical terms for auditionees prior to their callbacks and cold readings at the Colorado Shakespeare Festival in 1979: "Acting comes down to this: Who am I? Where am I? What's just happened to me either in the recent past or in the not-so-recent past—but that's very important because that conditions how you feel at this time. What do I want? And how am I going to get it? That's the whole excitement of acting. It comes spontaneously at the time when you meet the other person and the other person says, 'No, you can't have it,' and you then try to get it. And you may have to bully, yell, scream, plead, cry, or whatever you have to do in order to get what you want."[4]

When Molière's Arsinoë wants "to insult" Célimène in *The Misanthrope* (the character's intention), does she begin with a smile ("to trick") and then a casual remark ("to hint") and then follow up by crossing behind her and delivering a series of mild accusations ("to dig") before facing Célimène and giving her the real zingers ("to dump on")? These are some sample intentions which help an actor play the monologue. When you can identify a character's intentions, moment-by-moment objectives, and concrete actions, then you have something solid to perform onstage that gives your audition more power and greater interest.

Objectives come in two basic forms, internal and external. For example, Arsinoë may simply wish to hear herself talk or to plant suspicion or to parade her knowledge (internal/psychological goals). She may, however, want to provoke Célimène to anger or to disturb her physically or to discover Célimène's list of callers (external goals). It helps to distinguish between the two so you can devise a clear pattern of physical and verbal actions that are appropriate. In the above illustrations an actress might locate an action by devising some long crosses around and downstage of the imaginary character to "parade her knowledge" while speaking; or she may gesture pointedly and arrogantly with a fan at certain points in order to "disturb her physically."

Obstacles can be assigned in much the same way, internally and externally. Perhaps Arsinoë's speech is somehow forced or pointed because of an external obstacle (the social conventions of politeness and manners which Arsinoë is required to observe) or an internal one (her caution to conceal certain information from Célimène while insulting her). Again, you don't need to invent or discover anything complicated; the best choices are always the simplest and most basic onstage. An obstacle may be as simple as a character's fear of failure (Claudio's reluctance to speak to Desdemona about the punishment Othello has inflicted upon him) or even a physical defect mandated by the script (Laura's limp in *Glass Menagerie).*

Why are obstacles so important? Dramatic characters are never permitted to move towards their goals unimpeded—without some conflicts along the way. In everyday life, of course, our obstacles are rarely "dramatic," and that's why strong playing of obstacles is so important for acting and auditioning. They energize the scene by intensifying the struggle, by raising the stakes of the conflict. This is something that helps grip the spectator's attention (as well as the director's) just as it also feeds the audience's expectations. "They're all vampires out there!" Aaron Frankel points out about spectators and their gut reactions. "They come to the theatre because things are so much more alive there, because their own lives are incomplete. They want to feed on you because of your vitality—your blood courses so much hotter and fuller than theirs. That's why they're vampires."[5] Learn to work goal-and-obstacle combinations into your scenes and monologues so that your audition moves with punch, with urgency from the very first moments.

A handy way to begin looking for goals, obstacles, and actions is by asking yourself what changes by the end of the monologue or scene. What has developed, come to light, or happened? Does the character finish the scene by doing anything? By realizing anything? By changing an attitude toward a problem or by reaching a decision? Ask yourself too what difficulties might stand in the way of that process? Then you can nail down specific concrete actions to play moment by moment in order to bring the character to life. Always choose the most urgent objective for your audition piece, the most tenacious obstacles, the most concrete and basic actions.

Exploration 8: Goals, obstacles, and actions

Examine the speech by Launcelot Gobbo from Shakespeare's *Two Gentlemen of Verona* in the Appendix. Launce's final line suggests that the character's intention in the speech is to persuade his listeners that he's a good and generous master. Always describe characters' intentions and objectives by using infinitive phrases. Then you might sharpen this by saying that Launce wants "to win approval" from his listeners. Now, what obstacles must he overcome? Well, one general obstacle might certainly be his listeners' ignorance. The audience doesn't know how Launce educated Crab, how he had to put up with Crab's awful table manners, how lately he had to endure Crab's pissing under Milady's table, and finally how Launce took Crab's beating on himself. The result? Launce must painstakingly explain each of these points to his listeners. He must play each separate objective fully and distinctly, and they will be in sequence to lead the thought through the speech. He will "plead," "brag," "dump," "rage," or "cry" alternately at different points in order to do it—"to win approval." These are concrete four-letter verbs which tell an actor just what he's doing each moment.

Thus the character's goal in speaking has four smaller objectives connected with it, all of which lead up to an expression of "meaning" that the audience will derive. Don't worry about what the monologue means when you're thinking it through—that's the audience's job or the critic's. You just make choices to play certain actions that express the truth of your character's intentions as you, the actor, see them. The rest is up to God and the imaginations of the onlookers. In a two-character scene you can follow the same procedure, but find the obstacles by the patterns in the conversation. The give and take of dialogue, the changing subjects, the questions and comments all point to the major steps your character takes on his way to achieving his objectives.

Turn now to Johnny's speech from *No Place to Be Somebody* that you paraphrased in Exploration 3. Use the intention "to kill Sweets" as a starting point. Begin by listing the psychological obstacles holding Johnny back: perhaps his old loyalty to Sweets, his fear of getting nabbed, his confused emotions. Practice the speech by switching these obstacles in order to see which ones work best. Then devise a list of concrete actions that fulfill the objective. Maybe verbal ones work best for you, like "to shock Sweets" or "to brag" or "to mock," or physical actions such as "to poke the gun in his ribs" or "to circle him like a cat."

Repeat this exercise using Puck's speech from *Midsummer Night's Dream* in the Appendix. When rehearsing it for different obstacles, use the intention "to find and trick" the young Athenian. Possible obstacles might include his inability to see at night, his curiosity about the sleeping lovers, or a potion container that is stuck shut. Each of these might suggest specific actions to play. When you've rehearsed the speech exploring obstacles and actions in this way, then change the intention and rehearse again. Possible intentions might be "to reconcile the lovers" or "to dump on humans" or "to obey my master's orders."

Derive goals, obstacles, and actions from the context of the entire scene. In a cold reading of a play that you don't know or a new script, you may have to invent them. Once again, always choose the strongest goal, the most tenacious obstacle, the most concrete one-syllable verb as an action in order to make the scene vivid and convincing. The simpler you play these moment-by-moment actions the richer and more clear your performance will become. Work through your selection in this way until you're certain that you're playing it for its full potential, for all that it's worth.

The fourth step in preparation is to mark the pattern of actions in your script. Divide the speech or scene into beats that are the smallest significant units of dramatic action in the piece. Just as plays are often divided into large blocks of action called acts, and each act contains identifiable subsections called scenes, so too each scene (or monologue) must be broken down into its significant parts called beats. By playing these beats one by one you communicate the stages of your character's development more clearly to the audience, and your scene takes on artistic shape. This is extremely important in a brief audition because the pattern of beats that you establish and play will have a great influence upon the decisiveness and power of your performance.

If you have studied your goals and obstacles properly, you already know what the principal beats are. By rehearsing yourself to attack each goal when it first occurs, you'll be able to "punctuate" the sections of the speech or scene. Draw a line across the page between the words where one objective ends and another begins. Your actions should also change at these points. Launce's speech should have three lines (or four beats) to it, as indicated in the Appendix. Notice how each beat has an infinitive key phrase beside it that is simple and concrete, so that you can easily keep it in mind as you rehearse.

Exploration 9: Beats

Using Launce Gobbo's speech (Appendix) as a model, work through your two speeches now by Johnny and Puck. Draw lines (always in pencil) across your script where you see the character's objectives, concerns, or interests change significantly. Remember that you're establishing a pattern of what your character's thoughts might be underneath the words. Each beat you identify must be played differently, attacked strongly when it begins, much like bold lines on a painter's canvas.

The pattern you develop will show the auditors the major outlines of your character. Remember too that more than one pattern might be psychologically or artistically consistent; some experimentation in rehearsal will be needed in order to make a final decision. Then, beside each beat, "boil down" the objective of that section into a single infinitive phrase, a key-word phrase you can keep in mind as you rehearse. Each should be vividly expressed, as concrete as possible, and as distinct as possible from the preceding phrase in order to get maximum contrast into the audition.

You should work at first towards playing one, and only one, clear action at a time, and only when you've mastered this should you try to connect those single actions into a developing pattern for the entire scene. This will be your "final score" and will represent the interpretation of the scene and its character relationships. Build your monologue piece by piece systematically, and you'll make more progress than by simply playing it intuitively ("winging it").

It is at this point in your rehearsal process that your piece should begin to come alive. As you strengthen your playing of each beat to its full potential you will find yourself creating contrasts, vivid turns of thought, surprising discoveries, powerful conflicts. Give in to this sort of theatricalizing and let yourself go in the direction of playing that beat dynamically,

playing that action confidently for all it's worth. As one educational theatre director commented, "The single most common mistake of student actors at auditions is not going far
enough with the choices they've made—not playing contrasts
vividly, or changes in mood and in pacing."[6]

You have to keep in mind, though, that each beat is part
of the pattern. It's always a temptation for unskilled actors
to punch the strongest moment of conflict in the scene without
much thought to fitting that moment into the shape of the
scene as a whole. This makes for uneven acting, cheap thrills
derived from "pulling out the stops" when it's easy to do so.
You'll certainly decide to modify your interpretation later on,
but with a clear sense initially of how the pattern of a scene's
rhythm unfolds you'll be able to modify your intensity later
without trouble.

You'll find that these two selections by Johnny and Puck
present rich possibilities of interpretation. For example, Johnny's impassioned speech seems to be angry and desperate on
the surface, but recall Liv Ullmann's advice about showing
the opposite side of things. Modulate Johnny's anger by finding less-than-desperate objectives for some of the beats.
Weaken the character here and there as you rehearse and
discover more variety. Puck's speech, on the other hand, is
much less urgent; it's more playful, whimsical, filled with
discoveries. The beats change rapidly but the comedic potential in Puck's makes it as different from Johnny's as night is
from day. The character is a fairy spirit, and your performance
can shift quickly and unpredictably from one thought to another, from one turn to the next as the speech develops.

Voice

The fifth and final step in interpretation is to stage the piece
with effective voice and movement. Using the information
you've just obtained from paraphrasing, identifying obstacles, and marking beats, begin to search for vocal possibilities
to clarify and heighten the sense of the piece. There are two
helpful methods of doing this with your monologues. The

first approach involves going through the piece and identifying what are called the "operative words" in the sentence structure. An operative word is the most important word in the phrase or sentence, the one that should carry the most emphasis as you speak. To some extent, your success in this area is dependent upon your general literary sensitivity: your ability to read something in order to convey what is being said, to know what must be stressed, or to use subordinate phrases and modifiers in order to explain the point at hand.

In some cases the operative word is easily recognized and can be stressed with little difficulty by means of volume, pitch, or pauses because you're familiar with basic English sentence structure. You know, for example, that the object of the preposition usually carries the important meaning; you'd never say, "Now is the winter of *my* discontent." But you're also aware that knowing this is no guarantee you'll be able to do it consistently under the stress of performance.

Look at the speech by Muffet from Wendy Wasserstein's play *Uncommon Women* in the Appendix. There's a great temptation here for an actor to "rush" the opening lines, because the ideas are so familiar and so comically expressed, or for an auditionee to change the stress on certain words simply out of nervousness or in order to achieve variety with a long-rehearsed speech. It happens all the time in stage performance, and it drives directors crazy. The reading might sound something like this: "I am so tired. *Why* doesn't someone *just take me away* from *all this?* Did you ever notice how walking into Samantha's *room* is like *walking into a clean sheet?* She and Susie Friend *celebrate Piglet's birthday.*" Some basic operative words, however, that could be stressed for a more clear delivery are *take-away-sheet-birthday.* You only clutter up your acting by sloppy, indiscriminate emphasis which tells a director that you're not really on top of what the character is saying and feeling.

In addition to this "mechanical" basic method of spotting operative words, you need to develop an intuitive method that helps you choose which words are most important when the syntax is ambiguous. Some coaches refer to this as the "brown cow" exercise because it works just like the old cliché about oral interpretation: say "How now, brown cow?" four times, stressing a different word and changing inflections each time, noticing how the meaning changes or disappears altogether. Looking at just the first two lines of Muffet's speech, we can see how an auditionee's chosen emphases can say very different things about her character. "I am *so* tired. Why doesn't *someone* just take me *away* from all this?" Or "I am so *tired. Why* doesn't someone just *take* me *away* from all this?" The first stress pattern shows a weaker, more defeated character than the second, which might be spoken by the same character who also has the pluck, the anger, or the determination to do something about her situation. It's not just a matter of meaning—the audience will find a meaning either way. It's more a matter of clear, persuasive, focussed meaning that is always more effective on stage. For an audition, the second interpretation is preferable because it is a stronger, more dynamic choice to play. Locate the key operative words—especially verbs—and play them strongly.

Once you have identified the operative words, practice rehearsing your speech over and over until you're able to repeat the pattern of stresses more or less consistently. Use a tape recorder to help you, or have your coach or classmates listen only to the stress pattern in your voice as you perform the selection. Either method will enable you to discover where your delivery is emphasizing words that are better left unstressed or where your vocal emphases are inconsistent from one performance to the next.

Exploration 10: Operative words

The second copy of your speech will now be used for scoring the physico-vocal elements of your interpretation. Using a pencil, go through the text underlining the obvious operative words in each sentence: prepositional objects, active verbs, and the like. Then go through it again looking for ambiguities, places where stress is called for but where the syntax gives you no clear indication of this. In each case choose what seems to be the most important word(s) and underline again. Finally, go through the speech looking for unusual length or complexity in the syntax: parenthetical statements, numerous adjectival or adverbial modifiers, words in series, subordinate phrases—wherever you have a hard time sustaining the thought or making sense of long involved sentences. Select operative words here less upon the basis of their inherent meaning and importance than upon their value to the listener in making clear the sense of what is being said.

This last situation is the one requiring the greatest skill of the actor, as anyone who has had to perform Shakespeare realizes. You must carefully weigh the three or four principal parts of a sentence, gather your phrases, and establish a pattern of relative stress for each that will make the entire sentence complete in its sense and make its individual parts clear and meaningful in support of that sense. Although Shakespearean drama is well known for this type of syntactical complexity (and that is why Shakespeare is used so frequently in basic acting classes), the problem is not at all confined to older plays. T. S. Eliot, Bertolt Brecht, Edward Bond, and Peter Weiss are only a few modern playwrights noted for their skillful use of complex language, often in verse, and you'd do well to get a handle on this problem early in your training.

Once you've moved through your speech underlining the key operative words, the final step is to simplify the pattern. See if you can eliminate any of your underlinings and still retain the necessary emphases you wish to establish. Look carefully at your long sentences or at sections where more than one short sentence is used to develop a single idea to see if your underlinings succeed in carrying on or supporting the sense. Can you make do with fewer operative words in these sections? Examine the section of Muffet's speech (Appendix) beginning with "I guess the truth" and concluding with "even a few princes." Can this section build in a psychologically convincing manner by stressing only *truth-men-you-Holly-Samantha-always-attractive-shallow-impressive-really-prince-few?* Could you devise a different pattern using even fewer operative words? Work through your own speech like this, erasing unnecessary underlinings. Be certain that the opening few lines of your monologue have strong operatives, but don't drill yourself yet on performing it as a final interpretation.

The second helpful method for testing the vocal demands and potential of your monologue is by working with vowel and consonant sounds. You've undoubtedly worked before with gibberish improvisations that use no words but, instead, force you to convey meaning by phrasing, by increasing/decreasing volume and pace, and by changing the inflections of nonsense sounds. While gibberish can be used to prepare a speech, a more effective variation for auditions is to explore your monologue by forgetting for a moment the sense of the words and concentrating instead upon two specific types of sounds which the words contain: the consonants that ordinarily convey at least two-thirds of the meanings in our everyday conversation and the vowels that act like rivers flowing between and connecting consonants as well as controlling the emotional tone, the rhythm, and the overall shape of the speech.

Exploration 11: Stretching sounds

Begin by speaking the selection very slowly: lengthen each vowel sound and stretch the words like rubber bands.[7] Pronounce each and every syllable and exaggerate the use of your lips, teeth, tongue, and jaw as you speak in slow motion. You should feel like a big, fat fish if you're doing this exercise correctly. Using your pencil, circle the words or phrases that seem to stand out because of their vowel sounds. Repeat the speech two more times, each time a little faster in order to note if the circled words still make good sense when you stress their tonal (vowel) values. Do the speech with consonant stress in the same manner.[8]

By this time, the second copy of your monologue should have many words and phrases underlined or circled. Now you must decide how to combine the operatives with the sound patterns into a meaningful overall shape. Are many of your operatives also circled? If they aren't, could they be? In most cases you'll find that their sounds or the sound pattern of the immediately surrounding words can be used for proper stress. Did the sound-stretching analysis reveal any words that you overlooked earlier as strong operatives?

Work through your monologue by "composing" its vocal score according to these two basic methods. As you proceed you may also want to add markings for intonation, accents, pauses, and pace. Do so. When you're satisfied with your interpretation, you should then rehearse it until you can speak it naturally and comfortably, while still retaining at least some of the patterned shape that your written analysis suggested.

Movement

You've now reached the point where you can work your monologues or scenes onstage. Numerous acting exercises and improvisations can enhance the movement aspects of an audition. You've probably encountered several methods in your classes or play rehearsals, and now is a good time to look back over your experience to see what you can use—what feels right for you. The following discussion explains some common approaches for warming-up and then improvising upon a written text and lays out a few principles to keep in mind as you rehearse. It does not provide a specific set of instructions about "how to" stage your monologue because any set "technique" will only produce a mechanical performance. Instead, you must discover your own blocking and business by improvisation, using a coach's advice in the final stages.

Begin first by looking for authentic impulses to physicalize the content of your monologue or scene. You aren't looking for blocking, you're seeking impulses to physicalize. Avoid setting any blocking or gestures at this stage, and try to discover only the physical-emotional connections you may have with your material. Five common starting points for this process are contained in the following exercise; they can be done alone or with a partner.

Exploration 12: Movement improvisation

1. Walk uninterruptedly in a wide circle or even at random while whispering the lines or speaking them softly. Let the words sink into you without adding much expression to

your delivery. Repeat the piece three or four times until physical responses to the text begin to surface. Then go with them.

2. Move in various directions at super-slow speed, delivering the text as in step 1 above. Grossly exaggerate line delivery and movements for three to four minutes until the text begins to flow smoothly together with the dancelike movement. Your physical actions can be either totally abstract or realistic and pantomimic; usually they will become some combination of the two.

3. Devise dance or gestural patterns in silence (no speaking at all) while someone else or a tape recorder reads the lines slowly to you. Remain motionless until an impulse to move occurs to you, then go with it. Even small muscular reactions are important in this exercise. The improvisation requires strong concentration, and it must not be forced. While it may not yield large moves or gestures at first, it will alert you to key ideas in the text that have some personal "resonation" within you.

4. On the basis of the text analysis you've done earlier, concentrate upon the possibility of one physical-vocal gesture that you feel expresses your character's general attitude towards life—his or her "life gesture."[9] The gesture may not be overtly performed in the scene or monologue; you should make the choice whether or not it actually becomes overt. Experiment with several possibilities until you hit upon one that feels right to you—one which seems to encapsulate the character's attitude most accurately. Then work the lines trying to base all movements upon this life gesture.

5. Move uninterruptedly throughout the rehearsal space, touching and physically contacting everything that is available (levels, props, furniture, walls, clothes, people, etc.). Use your whole body for establishing physical contact. In this exercise you may wish to bring to the surface key features of your connotative or subtextual paraphrase instead of relying only upon the spoken text.

Any of these methods can stimulate your physical expressiveness and point you in the right direction for further movement study. They'll cause ideas and actions to surface, just like "brainstorming" a problem. Once you've warmed up by exploring them for half an hour you should then be ready to tackle the practical staging problems listed below in a creative way, with plenty of ideas. A word of advice: "half an hour" means actually *doing* it, not just thinking about it. This is not brain work like chapters 1 to 3; most of what you get out of vocal-physical improvs will be determined by what your body puts in.

The second step in physicalizing your audition piece is to move closer to movements and gestures which are specifically connected to the text. Keep in mind that movements as well as vocal interpretations should never be entirely set. If voice and body have been properly warmed up and trained, they should be responsive to whatever direction you wish to take in actual performance. This is the basis of spontaneity, freshness, inspiration. *The rule of thumb is to be certain that you can perform your piece differently if called upon to do it again.* In fact, at cold readings auditors will frequently ask you to do just this if they liked your first reading. They'll want to see the character differently, perhaps, or see how you can take direction and "add" something, or just find out how well you can adjust under stress. So remain flexible within any movement patterns you develop.

Once you've warmed up with any of the five methods outlined above, try to isolate those blocking patterns, gestures, and moves which reflect and express the pattern of action you identified in Exploration 9: Beats. Each change in your character's intentions, each new objective your character discovers in the scene should be expressed by a physicalization of some sort. This will help you to attack and play new beats strongly and purposefully, something that is especially crucial in the opening moments of your piece. But don't overdo it with the physical business. When auditioning you'll have relatively few basic movement patterns to choose from due to the time limit and the absence of scenery—usually only a single straight-backed chair. You also want to avoid too much movement because a speech or scene works differently in an audition than as part of a play. You don't want to seem too "busy" or rushed because you've crammed so much into a couple of minutes. Economy is always the rule; quality not quantity is desired.

In addition to planning movement that reflects the pattern of dramatic action, you also need to physicalize the psychological and environmental circumstances as much as possible. Many coaches, in fact, like to begin all monologue interpretation from this point; you must find out if it works for you as an early or later step in preparation. In any case, you begin by identifying your character's emotional condition within the scene; and no matter which particular emotions you assign the character, you must be certain that he or she is under some kind of stress. He must feel some emotional urgency towards his situation; the environment and psychological circumstances must affect his actions in the scene. Perhaps he desperately needs to achieve one or more of his objectives, or he's unsettled about the seriousness of the problem and the frustrating obstacles he encounters, or perhaps even his own uncertainty and confusion have raised his anxiety level. Whatever you decide, find a strong, compelling reason why your character is doing and saying these things in your speech or scene.

This doesn't mean that you should devise bold, strong, agitated, or "theatrical" activities for your monologue or that you must rack your brains to include flashy business wherever possible. It means, rather, that you center your attention upon the *importance* that the outcome of the scene or monologue holds for the character. (This will also reduce your stage fright by channeling nervous energy into the dramatic situation.) You must find some personal way of connecting with your character's concerns in the scene and believe absolutely in the importance of these concerns.

Directors and coaches sometimes call this "making the strongest choice possible." By identifying or inventing serious stakes for your character in the monologue, you can uncover many ideas for body energy, movements, and gestures that intensify your performance and reflect the dramatic issues. Following are some basic ways of achieving this sense of urgency in a scene.

Exploration 13: Physicalizing situation

1. The most common approach is also the most general in terms of method—mentally running over the given circum-

stances immediately preceding your entrance and "feeling" what your character would feel as a result of them. Where is your character coming from offstage, and what has just happened to him? What spaces has he just passed through and what (if anything) has just occurred there? Was your character reading, sewing, washing, crying, writing, etc? Some of this may be indicated by the script, or you can invent a brief biography in order to get yourself "into character" before beginning. The actual "moment before" you begin is especially important because it will help to propel you into the first few lines. If this approach works for you, then set two or three key images in your mind that, when recalled immediately prior to the audition, can quickly "trigger" the necessary emotional and physical state.

2. You can also focus upon sensory details that affect your character's moods and feelings during the scene in order to heighten your playing. Does your character have any immediate physical responses that you can use to increase belief in the situation? Is he cold or hot? Is he hungry? Does he have a headache or an upset stomach? Is he carrying anything onstage or fidgeting with hands or clothing? Is he comfortable or self-conscious about the way he's dressed, or the furniture and objects in the room, or maybe even the space itself? Run down the list of your five senses to identify or invent details about touching, tasting, hearing, seeing, or smelling that might help to give you a greater sense of involvement in the imaginary situation. When you've turned up a few possibilities, recall incidents from your own life when similar things affected your own behavior. Use these "sense memories" of your own to substitute for those required by the scene. Again, you should set two or three of these personal sense memories in your mind and use them to quickly trigger the necessary belief in the dramatic situation before you begin. They may also suggest concrete physical actions to play in performance.

3. You can concentrate simply upon the setting and work from there. For example, you can use the given locale but visualize it as a setting that you know—one that you've seen or lived in, or even your own room if possible. This is obviously good advice because the more familiar your imaginary scene, the more truthful will be your response to it and the less attention will be required in order to create it in your

mind. Be careful that a "familiar" setting doesn't become too familiar: comfort and security are not always appropriate feelings for characters in many types of monologues.

4. You can approach the physicalization of your piece by consciously inventing a new, emotionally charged setting to which your character would respond very strongly, one that heightens and is connected to the dramatic action before you even begin to verbalize. The famous acting teacher, Uta Hagen, recommends that you "determine what you are doing there *besides* talking to yourself. . . . You do *not* come into a room in order to talk to yourself. You do *not* sit down or rise to talk to yourself."[10] For example, where does the scene with Launce from *Two Gentlemen* take place and what is Launce doing there? Perhaps it could be a courtyard with other guests standing around or a public street with passersby. Launce might then be brushing the dust from his pants and feeling the sticky wetness of his shirtsleeve where Crab has just peed and at the same time trying to talk to one person or another in order to explain everything.

Communication

Uta Hagen's advice points us to the single most important question you must answer if your audition is to pack a wallop: Why is it important to you, as an actor, that these words be spoken? Uta Hagen reminds her students that a reason must be found for all a character's words and actions, that the character must speak out, must say these particular words at this particular time. And the same is true for you as an auditionee: the director wants to see you make choices—important ones—about the piece you've prepared. It must be special to you or it will never become special for the casting director. Without that "something special" your audition will seem at best correct or adequate—and that's another kiss of death in a casting situation.

Michael Shurtleff refers to this in two good chapters on a scene's importance and a character's humor: "Plays are written about the most important moments in people's lives," he insists, "not about their everyday humdrumness. . . . What an actor must look for in a play is something unusual. Something important." For the auditionee this can often mean finding humor in the character: "That attitude toward being alive without which you would long ago have jumped off the Fifty-Ninth Street Bridge."[11] You must unearth what really makes your character click in this scene and keep it in mind as you rehearse and perform. Why is it absolutely essential that he achieve his objectives? Try to identify with that need—to own it and believe in it. Actress-director Angela Paton compares this urgent need of the actor with the work of a novelist or painter who can create without an audience. "The actor *needs* someone to listen," she explains. "He *needs* to reach out off the stage and get a response. It should seem as though he could not *not* express his thoughts."[12] She suggests that when you rehearse a monologue, you visualize the responses you're getting from the imaginary character—that you seek immediate, direct feedback from your words and somehow tap into your character's eagerness to relate, to connect, to express himself to the other characters and the audience. So fight for your listener's attention; play your choices earnestly to win understanding and support from the audience and from the director.

As you experiment with movement patterns and learn to use the space for expressing reactions, pursuing objectives, establishing relationships, and the like, try to keep the following basic guidelines in mind.[13]

Exploration 14: Checklist for staging

1. Always face downstage in your introduction, in the pauses between pieces, in performance, and at the conclusion. This will give the auditors maximum opportunity to look at you; they're not interested in your back.

2. Search for ways to open out the scene or monologue to the audience, but under no circumstances should you play directly to the auditors. Allow them their distance and their anonymity in order to judge you objectively. They're not spectators, they're employers. Don't put them on the spot by demanding some sort of immediate reaction from them.

3. Always locate real or imaginary characters downstage

of you (never upstage yourself). In a two-character scene you'll need to modify this rule somewhat, but you must be sure that at all times you're more visually prominent than the other actor.

4. Ignore all stage directions in the script because you need to start afresh, totally adapting your selection for a different purpose and minimal setting. Some stage directions from two-character scenes can be helpful when they deal with character psychology or with the playwright's interpretations, but instructions for handling props, moving around the set, or performing business are largely useless for auditioning.

5. Play the monologue or scene as far downstage as possible, though you must always leave a comfortable distance of about fifteen feet between you and the directors.

6. If there are more objects in the audition space than simply a chair, by all means use them. Even in a prepared reading you can adjust your blocking and business slightly so that you can be seen working around furniture. Contacting material objects can also help to steady your nerves.

7. Experiment with a small hand prop as part of your audition. Did you ever see Humphrey Bogart as Captain Queeg in *The Caine Mutiny*? He constantly played with ball bearings in one hand. Michael Leibert of the Berkeley Repertory Theatre suggests that even something as simple as a matchbox can add color to a character's personality and help to ground the actor. Secondary activities like playing with a key chain, a watch, or a coin might take the monologue into a whole different world and give you a stronger connection with the material.

8. Always rehearse with a single chair, devising as many ways as possible for integrating it into the scene or monologue. You can locate another character in it, sit in it (though never longer than a few seconds), move around it, move it, or gesture with it—but use it.

9. Rehearse your scene under several different lighting situations so that you learn how to find and play the light in dim areas.

10. Rehearse your introduction and your "verbal resume" so that you feel comfortable speaking informally or answering questions from the director. Many young actors show great

skill eliminating personal mannerisms from their prepared selections, only to find that common questions like "What have you done before?" suddenly throw them into an anxious state of fidgeting or frozen immobility or facial tics. Practice talking about yourself with confidence and ease.

Working with a coach

At some point in your preparation, especially for graduate schools, scholarships, and summer work, you'll need to work with a coach. Ideally this should occur in the final stages because you have to discover by yourself some personal importance, some imaginative impulses on your own. There are four things to look for in a good coach:

1. Choose someone who loves to act and seems to know something about it.
2. Choose someone who understands and is willing to devote time to supervising all your "administrative" preparation (applications, choosing theatres, etc.).
3. Choose someone who is willing to work with you on a regular basis, at least twice weekly for a month.
4. Choose someone who is willing to help you out as a reference, as a person with outside contacts, or as a study director.

The first pointer is obviously the most crucial and the rest of this chapter deals with problems related to it.

At the onset of this chapter I stressed the need to work on your own because I think college students rely too much on their teachers—and the institution—to solve many of their problems for them. This is especially damaging for theatre students because so much of their success, both in school and afterwards, will depend on their strength as self-reliant and disciplined persons.

You are going to be selling your total self. You need to have fun with your training, to enjoy your work so much that you don't have to depend on others to get turned-on to it.

As Eric Morris and Joan Hotchkis point out in their book on professional acting, the actor's ability to take responsibility for his own life, to become self-motivating "is not just a way of working, it is a complete philosophy and a way of life. . . . You, the artist, will develop the totality of your own individual statement."[14]

It's absolutely essential for you to learn how to develop the "individual statement" that fulfills and expresses itself through your work and to begin this process early in your training. It's a never-ending process. By learning to work on your own you'll tap that creative spark within you. When you audition, it will be that individual stamp, those personally meaningful choices that will give your acting the authentic inner life directors are searching for. You must create this for yourself because no coach can give it to you. This is not to say that acting "honestly" will land you the role every time; the director may be seeking a different inner quality than the one you show, despite the belief and sincerity you bring to the reading. But without a solid groundwork (which means "homework") in self-discovery, belief, and personal commitment to your audition, few directors are likely to trust you to commit yourself to a role in their production.

In light of this you need to keep two things in mind when working with a coach: (1) be certain that you've done a whale of a lot of work on your own before you get coaching and (2) hang on to the personal self-discoveries you've already made as you add your coach's suggestions. Ideally the coach will give you time, honest observations and assessment, support, and suggestions for developing the best of what you have to offer. More often, though, you may find your coach trying to impose some sort of "standards" on you or pushing you to play the piece the way she or he might like to play it, or even using you to shape the piece according to what she thinks it ought to communicate—all of this without regard to what is appropriate for you as a unique person, what you have found personally meaningful, and then building on that.

If you can work up a good foundation on your own so that your coach's comments won't completely muddle your interpretation, and if you're certain that your coach isn't trying to impose on your performance something which doesn't feel right to you—doesn't express what you want to communicate—then you're probably ready with a solid base of confidence and trust to move ahead and begin polishing. Whatever you do, avoid falling into the "obedient student" trap with your coach; this is something that is hard to do for student actors. Perhaps you should consider this little piece of advice from the actor William Redfield, since "taking direction" from someone will be a problem you'll encounter in more than just auditions situations: "One need neither argue with a director nor 'take' direction with unquestioning, childish obedience. A proper instruction, carefully worded, would be: *Digest* direction. Be in or out of agreement, as your intuition dictates, but *listen* to the direction. If you don't like it, don't do it, but taste it, savor it—roll it about in your mouth. Then swallow it, digest it—it may work out. It may stretch you to an achievement you did not imagine. Do not confuse stubbornness with integrity. Be blown by the wind. Imagine yourself a kite."[15] Keep in mind that it'll be you up there onstage, not your coach, and that you'll have to feel completely comfortable with your presentation if it's to come off well.

You'll only look foolish if you try to fake what isn't real for you, so stay within your range. As Redfield points out, though, this does not mean that you should play it safe, cop out, and avoid taking risks. Any good acting teacher should be able to see what else the piece needs or what else you may have to offer and push you in that direction. That's not a threat, it's a challenge, and it's worth a shot to reach for it. But the bottom line is always what you think you can do well in performance.

Lead with your strength

The first thing you need from a coach is to learn where your strengths and weaknesses are. Your coach may already have some idea of this, but run your audition by her or him and ask for immediate gut responses. This is what audiences and directors will be doing too. You want to know what kind of attitude you project from the stage: does she think your reading was hesitant or aggressive? Quiet and timid or confident and bold? Maybe your coach will note nervous tension when you were shooting for "well-preparedness" or perhaps what seemed correct and carefully thought out to you came across to her as mechanical and lacking guts.

Obviously you want to work on or eliminate the negative qualities, but a coach's task isn't just to spot weak points, he or she should also give you support by noting good points too (many coaches fail to do this). Try to shape your audition so that you lead off with your best qualities. Are you good with comedy or just naturally funny to look at? Then kick off with your comic piece and work some humor into it early. You can even ask yourself if the piece still seems good comic material and change it if you think it's not. Is there a section in your serious piece where your coach felt you were connected strongly, something utterly believable? Emotionally authentic? Then ask yourself what your character's concerns were at that point and why you related to them. Find other sections where similar concerns were evident so that you can connect there as well. Your good points may be comic potential or emotional truth, as in these examples, or they may be charm and likeability, suppressed energy, honesty, simplicity, or something else.

Energy

Be sure that you're having fun with your audition and that your coach can see this. If he or she thinks you're not enjoying yourself, then stop right there and find out why, because no amount of technique will compensate for lack of enthusiasm. You'll never get anywhere at an audition without enjoyment: it's the basis of spontaneity and imagination. When you feel great about what you're doing, then your whole instrument responds—body, voice, energy, facial expression, everything. This is why it's so important to pick material that you can get into, something that's a part of you. And when you've rehearsed it and enjoyed playing with it, when you can identify with the character's concerns and really live out that situation for a few minutes onstage, *then* your acting becomes compelling to directors.

This is by far the hardest aspect of your audition to work at because there are no shortcuts to generating instant involvement, and yet this, above all, will have a solid impact on your listeners. "It's that swiftness of attack they look for," says Robert Goldsby, a West Coast producer-director. "It's a kind of energy—what the French call 'verve'—the presence the person shows right from the top of the audition. And there are all sorts of ways of getting that: emotional recall, sense memory, moment before, countdown—whatever seems to work best for a person. But it's got to be there."[16]

I like to remind my workshop students of the problems faced by screen and TV actors who have to repeat a moment several times while the director changes the camera angle or the lighting in order to capture the scene better. The actor must "be there" right at the top for the third or fourth take, with no lead-in time. Len Cariou, a seasoned professional with a raft of Best Actor awards for playing title roles in *Sweeney Todd, Applause, A Little Night Music,* and others, points to the importance of this skill that he learned in repertory work: "It's marvelous training. It serves well in making movies and working in television. You have so much starting and stopping, but I've had no difficulty sustaining a character. A good actor shouldn't. It's part of his responsibility."[17] Screen actor Paul Muni also points out that "the actor must make the additional effort of mentally coordinating his lines before the camera. He must be ready to reorient to the state of the scene preceding the one now being shot, and absorb it effectively so that his work will show the proper emotional development."[18]

You, too, must be able to plunge into your audition with only a second's preparation. Perhaps you'll use a key word for "sensory recall," some kind of physical centering before kicking-off or maybe a key image as a personal substitution for the mood of the scene. But that enthusiasm and fire to begin, that eagerness to fight for your opening goals from the very start of the piece, is extremely critical for the auditionee.

This starts, of course, from the first moment you enter the audition room. You are the most sensational performer those bleary-eyed directors have seen all afternoon. The opening lines of your monologue are vivid and arresting because you're eager and excited to perform them. And all the way through you are on top of what it is you want from the other character and from the audience. So you need to rehearse "making an entrance" and an introduction each time you perform your monologue for your coach. Never form the habit of just rehearsing the speech by itself, because your opening entrance to the stage and introductory remarks are part of the total audition, and often they can throw off experienced actors if they're managed badly. Have your coach drill you on doing this consistently and confidently.

Have the coach watch especially the opening lines of the monologue to see if that spark of enthusiasm is on tap, because after the first fifteen seconds the directors will be writing things down about you—pass or fail. And lastly, find out from your coach where the energy in your total audition seems to sag. It always will, of course; you can never get on top of that entirely. Try to focus your complete psychophysical alertness on anything for awhile and see what happens. Four-to-six minutes is a lot of time.

Who-What-Where

In addition to the energy level you bring to the audition, you need to sharpen your alertness, your awareness of the moment-by-moment playing of the monologue or scene. Generally professional coaches place the heaviest emphasis on three areas:

1. the relationships (of the character to himself, to the other character, and to the audience)
2. the objectives (the choices, goals, intentions, needs that define relationships)
3. the situation (the environment, the physical place and, by extension, the given circumstances or context)

These are easily remembered as the "who-what-where" determinants of a scene, and they should be used for all dramatic material.

With regard to relationships, the identity of your character should be clear (and I don't want to say too much about this because it's rather obvious). His characteristics should be clearly defined by your pattern of activities onstage, and his needs or attitudes towards the other characters and the audience should be apparent. This last point is extremely important. It means that you must work to gain the attention of the auditor, because if you don't, you'll be forgotten quickly after you leave. Your character absolutely must express himself at this moment in his life; he needs contact with others (just as you do), he needs to interact. Ask yourself why you (as the character) are saying these words and identify the strongest possible reason for communicating. Do you need the audience too? Of course you do. Why? And why do you need the other imaginary character (if there is one)? What does that person have to offer you? Where is the urgency to speak, the impulse to relate importantly, meaningfully? Who are you, and what are you doing to others onstage and to the directors in the audience?

Your coach should be able to feel your performance moving out of the playing area in order to establish this sort of dynamic contact. Perhaps your scene begins in a certain locale and then broadens to include the audience, the "world-at-large." Always beware of playing that fourth wall just at the proscenium line in an audition—move it to the back of the house and see what happens to the monologue or scene. Have your coach check to see if you're sharing your performance with the listeners. With an imaginary character, choose a vis-à-vis who is not a sympathetic listener but who forces you to communicate instead: perhaps someone who is ignorant, hostile, loving, or surprised. There should be several carefully chosen places where your "character" needs to reach even beyond the auditorium itself. Balance your performance so that your focus shifts between the stage characters and the public, because playing to only one is far less engaging for a director.

The motivation for this, of course, springs from the inner life of your character, the content of the words he is saying. As New York director Aaron Frankel reminds his acting students in performing Shakespeare: "Shakespeare provides the vehicle, but you supply the gas. You're the driver, and the words are there only to help you act on your impulses. If you really saw your Juliet, your action would be obvious and your ability to get there would be increased, and poor Juliet, you know, hardly could defend herself against the onslaught. That's what we're talking about."[19] Visualize your character, his situation, and the other character in the most concrete details possible, and then allow your inner impulses to take over and move you forward. Remember the advice about movement given earlier in this chapter: focusing upon your inner life without allowing yourself to respond physically is just as deadly as too much concentration upon blocking, gestures, and external technique without proper belief and motivation.

Point number two, playing objectives, is the way in which the relationships are actualized. It's what draws you to connect, to do what you do and say what you say in the monologue. Michael Shurtleff calls it "what you are fighting for" and the word "fight" is the operative one. You play your objectives sharply, you fight to win, you go for it and you "kick ass" to get it. Nothing stops you, from the first objective to the last. Obviously this doesn't mean that you crash through the scene like Godzilla. Different people have different ways of "strongly pursuing" their goals, and an emotional blitzkrieg is always the kiss of death at an audition. It does mean that you know what you're going for at each moment of the scene and that you consistently pursue that objective until a different one replaces it.

Playing goals consistently is one of the hardest things to learn to do. There is so much coming down on you at tryouts that is not connected to the dramatic material: you're distracted by backstage or auditorium noise, your nerves are shot, you are self-conscious, the stage-lighting and acoustical space are totally unfamiliar, the stage manager is timing you, the director is scrambling under the table looking for a pencil, and so on. Meanwhile, what's happened to the shape of the scene? You can see why developing the ability to concentrate is one of an acting student's most important tasks. Tighten down your presentation by eliminating unfocused activity and by making some basic choices about how you're going to play it. Be absolutely clear about your objectives: what they are and where they change. When you rehearse with your coach, try to discover where your playing seems "fuzzy" in terms of what you want from your listener (this may be the same place where your coach saw the energy beginning to sag). Use your coach to discover which actions are the most expressive, and junk those that are unnecessary, repetitive, or uninteresting. To do this you need to keep an eye on your objectives.

Point number three, the situation, refers broadly to the entire context in which relationships are established and goals pursued and which in turn influences those relationships and goals. It means the physical and psychological environment. No matter how strong the relationships you create by focusing upon the character's need to communicate, and no matter how consistently you believe in your character's objectives and play the actions, your performance will still lack meaning, concreteness, and focus unless your actions have been chosen to reveal the circumstances in which your scene or monologue is taking place. Your coach can help you decide whether your audition needs a little or a lot of attention to place, objects, and properties. He or she can also suggest ways of using them that you may have overlooked: as obstacles, as sources of tension or enjoyment, as functional possibilities for blocking and gesture, and so on.

Remember that "a little or a lot" means just that: some pieces may require minimal attention to the physical environment, as when your character's preoccupation is entirely bound up with internal needs, or vice-versa. Generally speaking, you will know when you need to play the actual physical place by references in the script (especially in the scene). Inventing a setting for your monologue can greatly enhance the energy and importance of your acting, as pointed out earlier in this chapter. Your coach can explore this with you. Together with strong actions to play and compelling relationships to establish, your belief in the concrete, given circumstances can help keep you alert and responsive onstage. The who-what-where is a handy rule of thumb at auditions.

Thus far we've looked at a coach's assistance in five basic areas of your audition:

1. overall strengths and weaknesses
2. enthusiasm

3. relationships
4. objectives
5. situation

You'll need to spend hours of time and energy working at these problems, but your skills should develop quickly if you stay with it in a disciplined and systematic way. To some extent, though, these are only the basics, and your coach will probably suggest more values that he or she feels you can bring out. This will depend on the coach's personal tastes, your capabilities, and the nature of the material.

In the Shurtleff method, for example, the three guideposts of "relationship-goals-the moment before" are primary, while the other nine operate only within certain kinds of scenes: Is there role-playing going on here? Is there some mystery concealed? Is there surprise? Other directors and coaches speak of "colors" or "threads" that run through the monologue—a progression of thoughts, images, and feelings that the character is expressing. Your coach may advise something as simple as a new blocking pattern that might be especially revealing or a touch of humor which might suddenly throw some character trait into bold relief. Only experienced coaches know how to add suggestions like these as part of your final polishing, and often they provide a fresh impulse for approaching the scene in a unique way. Be certain to explore these refinements and to enter the results of your coaching sessions in your journal. Remember that you should always have previous ideas digested when you come to each rehearsal and be ready to contribute something new of your own.

Staying fresh—going stale

Every actor reaches a point working on plays or audition pieces where the material seems overrehearsed. This is called "going stale in the part," and it takes many forms. If you regularly feel bored or uninspired about rehearsing or performing a piece, if your coach tells you repeatedly that it sounds mechanical, if your acting seems constantly sluggish, or if you just plain feel it isn't going anywhere—then you obviously need some techniques designed to uncover more possibilities to play. Don't be depressed about your moods. They happen to everyone. And remember too that you won't be able to predict your mood or feelings at the time you actually audition. Be ready to deal with this problem in rehearsal because it may very well occur in performance.

Every actor has his or her own way of dealing with this, and you must find yours. The following section provides six Explorations that can help you keep your pieces fresh. In combination with your preperformance warmups, they represent the "finishing touches" for preparing monologues or scenes.

Exploration 15: Staying fresh

1. *Pick-a-Place.* Rehearse your selections in unusual environments: a closet, an open field, a cemetery, an office, a classroom, the shower, a large auditorium, an intimate studio, a hallway, etc. In each location open yourself up to the influence of this new setting; let the environment work upon your piece and alter your performance from what may have been set. You may not know what the audition place is like until you actually walk into it—much less have time to rehearse in it. Acoustics, stage height, lighting, and spatial relationships are only a few of the unknowns you have to encounter. In rehearsal a new environment may also trigger fresh ideas for you. After a half hour of rehearsing in a new space, return to the original setting and circumstances and see what has changed.

2. *Pick-a-star.* In this exercise try to pull out all the stops and ham it up by caricaturing famous actors as you perform the monologue or scene. Try it like John Travolta or Woody Allen, or perhaps like Bela Lugosi in *Dracula*. What happens when you deliver the piece like a melodramatic heroine in one of Daniele Steele's novels? Or when you sing it as though it were an operatic aria or a shampoo commercial on TV? This exercise will certainly help to break down any dulling habitual patterns you may have unconsciously formed. The

operatic approach has often revealed vocal and emotional possibilities that my students overlooked on their own. Again, after a half hour of this, return to the original characterization, allowing any new impulses to surface and influence you as you rehearse.

3. *Pick-an-obstacle.* Give your character a strong physical obstacle to overcome as you perform the monologue or scene. Try your speech as though you had a couple of tomahawks buried in your back, as though you were searching the room frantically for a valuable piece of jewelry or fumbling with a stuck zipper. Perhaps a hunchback, a wooden leg, or some other specific ailment will help you to play the speech more urgently. The environment may also be used here—what happens to the speech when you and your partner are trying to free yourselves from huge gobs of sticky taffy or while trying to move through thick jungle vines or when crawling under-over-through furniture and other obstacles? Never include such arbitrary obstacles as permanent elements of your presentation, because they're obviously artificial creations for rehearsal purposes only.

4. *Abandonment.* There are many variations on this exercise, which basically involves nothing more than letting yourself go completely in any direction you may feel at the moment. This may mean thrashing about and writhing on the floor, kicking and screaming like a mad person while belting out the lines. In scene work, you and your partner can deliver each and every line by greatly exaggerating the intention behind it. Turn discomfort into hysterical paranoia, pleasantries into passionate avowals of love, disagreements into blind, screaming rage, questions into desperate pleadings, and struggle with your scene partner this way two or three times through. Often with monologues you can ignore the text completely and improvise your own words and sounds for the emotional lines set down in the speech as you flail about the rehearsal space, giving in fully to any impulse that strikes you. Having pushed the text as far as you can go, you can then return to the original piece with a greater feeling of relaxation and confidence.

5. *Candid Camera.* This exercise should be done when you're feeling comfortable with a monologue and is especially revealing as a test of your sincerity with the material. The

exercise consists simply of performing your monologue as a part of normal conversation with someone who doesn't know that it's an audition piece, perhaps a total stranger. Bus stations, bars, locker rooms, dormitory rooms, car trips—numerous situations can provide you with sufficient "given circumstances" to start talking with someone. Try to be convincing, and when you've finished, see if the other person has believed you. Obviously this exercise is suitable only for certain kinds of monologues, but when it is properly carried off it can yield valuable and interesting insights.

6. *The Audition Game.* This exercise is a group activity. It involves getting together with some of your fellow acting students to perform your auditions, to read each other's audition material, and to criticize each other as "directors" or "agents" or "choreographers." While working with a coach or performing for an acting class is also valuable, an informal group of friends can often be more supportive. You may find it easier to explore new ideas, to relax and release tension, to sustain your interest and enthusiasm when working on a common problem together on a regular basis.

All of these improvisations share one thing in common: they'll help keep you flexible no matter what kind of performance situation you may encounter. They should never be used in an actual audition, but the "spirit" of improv—spontaneity, choosing and responding honestly and immediately, risk-taking, and invention—should inform all of your acting, whether auditioning or performing in productions. Improv becomes especially important in developing skills for cold readings. Judy Jenkins of CBS casting in New York points out that most television auditions require the actor to read from scripts he's never seen before and that skill with improv is always beneficial: "Mostly what it gives you is a certain confidence in working without the printed page. Actors should know they have the talent to perform without script—without someone giving them Shakespeare or Shaw. Often you just have to read it, then get up and do it."[21] Robert Cohen agrees and suggests that you "try out your audition piece as often as you can in an acting class, at a party, in your home, . . . Get used to performing amidst general inattention and extraneous noise."[22]

Improvisational experience is not only helpful for developing cold reading skills; many directors, in fact, include improv as a part of the general audition. James Roose-Evans of Great Britain's National Theatre always includes improv as a part of casting: "I may have them stand on their heads and sing 'Rule Britannia' or 'Mary Had a Little Lamb' in the middle of a reading just to see how they take direction, work together, or perform under stress."[23] Jack Fletcher, director and coach with the American Conservatory Theatre, uses improv in casting and in teaching when "you can see that they're locked into a certain way of doing it that is inhibiting them from discovering more about the piece or from achieving a certain spontaneity. I make them get up and I totally change the given circumstances. I make them run around and do it, or I make them do it as a six-year-old child trying to get a piece of cake off the table—anything that'll trick them into shedding a preconception about the piece."[24] Finally, there is Jane Armitage, director of International Activities for the Drama Studio, who includes improv as one of five necessary parts of the audition for prospective students. "I can learn if they're willing to take risks," she observes, "if they can concentrate and react honestly, if they can fulfill their goals in the improv (can they take direction), and especially, can they deal with specific details: the place, the circumstances and so forth."[25]

From this point, you're on your own until the audition time. Pace yourself according to a regular schedule, practice self-discipline, and keep your journal up to date.

Chapter five

The Audition

It was the Russian actor Stanislavski who said, "Let him who cannot sense the magic threshold of the stage, not presume to cross it." I'm sure you know what this refers to. Usually it's the very moment before your entrance: waiting in the wings on the final line of a countdown between a tense backstage and a supercharged onstage. The moment you step into the set the magic happens—"you're on!" The threshold of the stage is very real to an actor, as real as cement.

But before this moment occurs, you've already stepped through other "thresholds" along the way: walking into the theatre and leaving your everyday cares behind, warming up in order to awaken your physical and imaginative responses, applying costume and makeup and staring into that developing mask of your character. What you've done is to move through a series of doors, each of which leads more narrowly towards the final goal of bringing that character alive onstage.

A disciplined actor will always follow a series of steps like these either consciously or instinctively as a means of "getting into character," and it helps young actors to think of auditioning in the same manner—as a series of stages (or even "beats" in your overall audition) that gradually lead to a one-to-four minute presentation. Let's look at these stages more closely.

The ritual of staying calm

The first step is your arrival: early enough to relax and to shed hassles about anything. You enter the audition space and check it out. Locate the stage manager and learn what the procedure is. Give your name or your resume or take a form and fill it out. Do whatever is necessary to register yourself at the event. This can be a formal or informal process. At regional auditions for summer work and graduate schools you may need papers, pictures, resumes, and confirmations to present, while at your school's play the stage manager might simply collar you, shove a form into your hand, and take your name.

While you're doing all this, take a look around you. Can you see the stage? What's it like? Where are the directors? Who are the other auditionees? What's the sound like in the space? Notice everything you can and attune yourself to the environment. This is a good basic exercise to perform even in a hallway, an exercise that will help your concentration and center your energies.

In most cases you'll find the stage area is closed to anyone who isn't staff, so that the directors can audition people in a more private, relaxed situation. But you should be able to get at least a glimpse into the audition room if you arrive early enough. Try to get into the space itself. Walk around and learn everything you can about it. The more familiar you are with the audition space—by mental or actual physical exploration—the more relaxed you'll be when you perform.

After your initial exploration, finish whatever needs doing to complete your check-in, find out how and where you're going to be called, and locate a place to warm up. This last piece of advice should be engraved inside every young actor's skull. Under no circumstances walk out in front of people to perform something without warming up. You'll never find a professional doing this, but young actors usually don't treat warm-ups seriously. It takes a lot of energy to perform well onstage; it needs to be on tap and to be aligned in order to work for you when your instincts call for it. Acting doesn't come naturally. Your physical, intellectual, and emotional resources need to be warmed up and integrated before you can perform well.

There's absolutely no excuse for failure to do this, because all drama students are exposed to warm-up exercises somewhere in school. The most common cop-out I get is, "There's no warm-up room we can use." If you ever attend professional auditions in New York or Los Angeles you'll find people crouched in stairwells, phone booths, broom closets, bathrooms—even using the street outside—warming up their instrument. They are hungry for a part. You can work your voice anywhere, but also try to do some movement if you've got the space. Certainly on most campuses there's a classroom or hallway or office vacant nearby where you can do your stuff for at least fifteen minutes.

Self-consciousness accounts for much of the reluctance to warm up at auditions. You've got to remind yourself to take your work seriously. You really want that role don't you? And an actor is supposed to perform for people, isn't that also true? So what's the special problem about an audition performance, or a "warm up" performance with people watching you (if you can't find some privacy)? The other watchers are already at a disadvantage, that's why they're watching you so enviously. They lack focus or they'd understand. Remember that whatever roles are to be assigned are going to be *earned* by a good audition. You must get your energy up by some actual preparation before you walk in front of the directors. Creative juices don't automatically flow, they must be summoned.

Take your warm-up ritual seriously, no matter which method you use. Singing scales, puffing through calisthenics, working at dance routines and exercises, doing line rehearsals (for prepared pieces), yoga—it really doesn't matter so long as you are:

1. shedding the trials and tribulations of your personal life outside the rehearsal hall;
2. increasing your awareness of your physical, emotional, and intellectual power;
3. raising the energy level in every part of your body, especially your voice (volume, breath support, and articulation);
4. running over the particular physical and vocal demands in your prepared pieces;
5. listening for your name to be called by the stage manager (*very* important).

At this point you'll need to get into your rehearsal outfit, part of which is also your audition costume. Always wear tights to an audition because you never know what you'll be asked to perform and tights heighten your physical awareness and body energy. Wear the tights with a leotard for dance auditions if those are being held separately. Over your dance outfit, complete the rest of your audition costume according to three basic rules:

1. wear something which permits comfortable free movement;
2. wear something memorable that will help you stand out in the director's mind when the time comes to cast;
3. wear something neat and appropriate.

What does the last point mean? On the one hand, a suit and tie will not help you, and on the other hand, tie-dyed overalls won't make it either. "Something neat and appropriate" can also be "memorable" if it communicates good taste, functionality, and attractiveness. The business suit, like the bib overalls, stamps you in a character type that's hard for a director to ignore at casting. For dance auditions an unusually cut or colored leotard is always good, though the same memorability can be achieved by add-ons like leg warmers, sashes, or scarves. Do your own thing, but always try to give yourself an edge. In large "cattle calls," attention to costume can tip the balance and jog a director's memory for a callback.

As for the rest, remember that you want to look serious about your work. Avoid high heels, platform shoes, and tennies. Be sure you can work in your clothes and that they show you're a person with self-respect. Directors have good taste, and they want to see actors who can dress professionally and appropriately, actors who are at home in their "costume" instead of being wooden. Clothes can do that to you. One reminder: if you get a callback, always wear what you wore at the general reading because a director's memory needs help.

One final thing to keep in mind about the audition is the

long wait before you're called. You might wait for hours at professional calls for summer theatres, and even for collegiate shows you'll be lucky if you finish in less than an hour. You know what happens to you when you've been kept waiting for a considerable period, especially when you're keyed-up for competition. You grow bored and impatient, your energy sags, and you lose the edge you came in with. The longer you're kept waiting, the more negative you tend to become toward the directors who are holding you up and toward the whole audition.

Don't let this happen to you. That attitude is certain death at tryouts. The only antidote is a positive outlook: nobody is "keeping you waiting." That's a "poor me" victim-trap mindset. The fact is there is no one to blame. The process takes a long time. Not too long ago, at statewide auditions conducted for professional theatres and graduate programs by a theatre association, so many auditionees turned up that the waiting lines were much longer than could have been predicted. The actors had to be told to reduce their three-minute selection to one minute!

There's no predicting what kind of situation you'll encounter at an audition, especially at the professional level. One thing you can be sure of, though, is that the directors are not wasting time, no matter what it may seem like to you.

So keep a healthy attitude. The casting people are making tough decisions, lots of them every minute, and they've been sitting there for hours trying their best to evaluate fairly every piece of talent that comes along. Give them a break by being on their side (directors hate to see sullenness, defensiveness, or downright antagonism). Try to help them make the best decision by being positive, alive, and eager when you get onstage in front of them. That counts.

Physical alertness will count. Stay ready with whatever methods you can find. You might have to do mini-warmups two or three times while you're waiting in order to keep your energy on tap. If you're sitting down and watching the readings, concentrate on the performances so you grow familiar with the material the directors are using. This is the advantage for those waiting to read; those called first get the directors when they're fresh, but those coming later have more time to criticize and prepare. If you're waiting outside the audition room, try to talk to actors coming out in order to learn what's happening inside: How much time are people getting before cutoff, what are the directors looking for, what kinds of scenes are being used. Are cold readings going on? Who are the casting people? Ignore advice on "how to do it"; try instead to learn the unknowns about what's going on so you'll have an edge on the unknown. Forewarned is forearmed.

The audition performance

At every audition you'll be presenting one extra character in addition to the roles you've been rehearsing—that extra character is yourself. I mentioned earlier that directors will automatically begin casting you from the moment they see you onstage, so thoroughly rehearse your entrance and introduction in order to seem as confident and professional as possible. It's this "you" that they'll cast. But it's only one part of your total performance that should have a planned shape to it. A well-rehearsed self-presentation shows that you know (and are confident about) who you are and what you're doing. It sells your seriousness of purpose to the directors.

Be businesslike about your four-minute activity onstage by remembering what you're about: an actor presenting different features of yourself at *all* times—not just with prepared dramatic material. A good entrance doesn't just help directors, it can help you too. Your remarks help you listen to yourself before launching into your performance; your placement of furniture and movement to your starting position or "mark" can help you feel out the environment. Stay aware of these things. Play your entrance fully by being sensitive to the space and your relationship to the audience. As you enter take a look at the lighting and immediately locate your fourth wall right behind the auditors. Set your chair, then come downstage as yourself and speak directly to the auditors when introducing yourself and your pieces.

Let's look more closely at some details of this self-presentation. I recommend the following scenario for a general audition:

1. Enter and set up.
2. "Hello. My name is *A* and I'll be doing two pieces for you today. The first thing I'd like you to see is the character of *B* in the play *XYZ* by *C*."
3. Go to your mark, take one beat to concentrate, then attack the first selection. Finish with a freeze, a gesture held for a beat or two, and some kind of "cap" as a stop.
4. "Thank you. For my second piece I'd like to show you *D* in the play *ABC* by *E*."
5. Repeat number 3 above.
6. "Thank you very much. My name is *A*."
7. Turn, collect your things, and exit.

This format gives you several advantages. First, it's brief and to the point; it doesn't waste a second. Second, it gives you some extra moments at the start to move around and speak comfortably as yourself. Third, by introducing each selection separately, you can end-stop the first and have a little break without having to rush right into your second piece. Finally, by repeating your name at the end you remind the directors who you are and "present yourself" one more time. You can modify this by adding a third dramatic or singing piece, or by allowing time before you exit to answer questions.

If you keep in mind this need to present that extra character—yourself—at the audition, you'll reduce your awareness of your own nervousness, heighten your projection, and strengthen the presentational "marketing" features of your audition.

A second reminder for performing a good general audition is to do it as rehearsed and avoid rushing. You'll find that nervous tension always produces nervous rushing. You've got to remember that the directors want to see feeling. They look for an actor's emotional and imaginative commitment to a situation or a relationship onstage; this doesn't mean getting to the end of the bloody thing as fast as possible—it's each step along the way that's important. The directors will be watching intently only for the first thirty seconds, at most. So you've got to work it moment-by-moment right from the start, feeling out the relationship or the image or the problem as you go along, not concentrating on the end of the piece at the beginning. Rehearse for this: avoid thinking of the beat coming up while you're supposed to be fully playing the beat at hand. Play each beat singly before following through to the next. This is especially important for playing scenes in musical theatre auditions, which we will deal with in the next chapter.

Part of this moment-by-moment playing under stress requires that you let yourself react honestly to the emotional punches in your material. Again, don't be so overrehearsed and wired-up that you play your peak moments mechanically for the directors. Pay attention, for example, to the ending moments of your pieces. Let the auditors see your "recovery" between selections and before your exit remarks. Make these transitions with emotional honesty and avoid cutting them off either technically (to get to the next thing) or self-consciously. It's another way of presenting your *self* at the audition. The recovery process is far more engaging to watch than an actor who's just setting up furniture for his next piece. Give yourself an edge.

As soon as possible after finishing the audition do a post mortem in your journal. Analyze your recital pieces: How well did they hold up for you? How were they received? How did they change from rehearsal? Discuss your reactions, too, paying special attention to your feelings of personal rejection and failure. How well did you manage to pass off the rejection (assuming you didn't get the part)? Did the auditors give you any feedback during or after your performance? Did they cut you off? And how did you react? Test yourself on how well you were able to treat the experience as a game, as an important and hard-fought business activity conducted according to given rules *in which nothing is ever taken personally*—by the directors or by you. And "personally" means whether you got a part ("Gee I guess she liked me") or whether you landed only a simple "thank you very much." In short, don't let success or failure at auditions go to your head or turn on your worry machine. Putting it all down in your journal gives critical perspective and will help you to handle future auditions despite the fear of rejection.

Cold readings

Virtually all directors I know (myself included) hate and de-
spise cold readings even though we use them constantly. We
are seeing an actor at a tremendous disadvantage and what
we can learn about his or her talent is arguable. Can the actor
read the words sensibly? Does her or his voice sound confident? How much does the actor tie himself to the book or get
away from the script to create some zing with a scene partner?
Can I fairly judge the actor's impulses to move and speak and
gesture well under these circumstances?

Cold readings are important to directors for three reasons:
they show how well actors work under pressure; they force
actors to use and reveal themselves as persons; and they bring
the play partially to life for the first time. Notice that I didn't
mention the skill of taking only five or ten minutes to create
a full-blown, believable character—a common misconception
among young actors. No one would expect this at a cold
reading, and don't demand it of yourself or the very idea will
petrify you. A complete transformation into a character can
emerge only after weeks of growth in rehearsals. Concentrate
instead upon meeting the three demands just mentioned.

Demand number one: realize that you're working under
pressure to perform, and that you should only make basic
choices about playing your material. Don't get wrapped up
in the psychological or literary complexities of the material
you're handed. That only wastes time. In a cold reading
you've got to avoid muddiness and clutter by finding simple,
clear, basic things to play. Any good actor will have some
immediate gut responses to cold material: so go with yours
when you're handed a scene to look over, and you'll find it
easier to generate enthusiasm. Be sure you read through the
lines aloud at full volume. Never waste time memorizing the
lines or rehearsing anything with your scene partner. Work
out *by yourself* what you're going to do—just as your partner
will—and then be prepared to act your choices (and react to
his) on the spot. Reading aloud will stimulate immediate responses to the material.

While you're rehearsing the cold material—usually a
scene—your mind will be working hard. What should you be

alert for? One approach is to immediately identify the kind of play it is: sitcom, melodrama, wild comedy, tragedy, sheer farce, and so on.[1] This way of keying into your material by "typing it" can help you to quickly pick out an appropriate energy level for playing it, a certain frame of mind or an attitude underlying all the lines and physical actions. "This is a scene of tense melodramatic conflict between mother and daughter" (the closing scene of *The Little Foxes*); or "This is a nervous, starry-eyed love-at-first-sight situation" (the opening Guenevere-Arthur scene in *Camelot*). One Broadway director calls this technique the "angle of vision, an outlook through a character's eyes from which to view the material."[2]

When you have only a few moments to prepare, settle on the way you're going to play it, and your performance will tend to be consistent and thoughtful as a result. These are plus points with directors because they spell focus, even if the interpretation isn't entirely correct. "What I first look for is imagination and instinct," remarks one West Coast director. "By instinct I mean a certain spontaneity in the work that, no matter how raw it is, says to us that this person is not really afraid of going with what their intuition is about any particular piece. . . . You can see something in their work that is charged with some sort of willingness to give over to what their unique instinct is about it."[3] If you can get on top of a scene's "style"— no matter how simply you conceive it—you stand a good chance of coming off as a vivid, interesting actor. Remember that a common and deadly impression at a cold reading is to appear to be "hesitant average."

A second way of dealing with the pressure of cold readings is to immediately decide upon your character's specific objectives in the scene, devise two or three concrete physical actions to express them, and then play the scene by pursuing those chosen objectives strongly and consistently from the outset. One acting coach explains this in her workshop as, "What is my dream? What am I fighting for? What am I going to do to get it?"[4] You should be playing this right from the start by concentrating upon an opening action that propels you into the scene, that makes the other actor need to do something: a "first attack" that will bring about conflict.

Find a strong assertive verb, something that will force

you into a relationship at the outset. This "moment before" a scene begins isn't the history behind it (though it may include some of the given circumstances if you know them); it's an immediate action. It should be an urgent, concrete problem, need, or goal that drives your character into and through the scene. Your attack on the scene should spring from something painful and urgent—something sticking you that you have to do something about, an itch you've got to scratch. Just before you begin, take a second's preparation to let the image take hold of you. Fix that assertive verb in your mind, then forget everything else and play the scene moment by moment.

Either of these methods—finding the kind of play it is or finding concrete actions—will quickly give you something to play under conditions of stress. They'll help you make decisions, and as Aaron Frankel says, decisions are the basis of acting. Decide, and then go for the decisions you've made. Drill yourself frequently on reading cold material both ways until you get the hang of working at it systematically. Acting is craft. The ability to create something original and vivid out of totally unfamiliar material is what cold readings are all about, and it's got to be automatic—like the ability to read storybooks to children.

Demand number two: generate belief in the given circumstances by personalizing them and using yourself. Be certain of course that you understand what's being said in the scene, the sense of the words that you and the other character are saying. Be certain, too, that you know the events: what happens, where the turning points are, where the changes occur. Never violate these givens as you speculate upon possible physical actions, objectives, or obstacles. But most important of all, use this information to create some authentic, personally meaningful relationship with that other character. The centrality of human relationships, like the element of conflict, is a universal feature of all dramatic material.

An actor's ability to do this in cold readings is based on his or her ability to personalize the reading by belief in the basic situation. This requires a great amount of emotional "honesty." It's easy to throw up a "character" on the basis of a few bits and pieces skimmed from the text, but that's just a mechanical exercise, and the character will almost always be two dimensional as a result. Use whatever you can discover about the given circumstances in the scene, and then place your self imaginatively into them. Ask yourself: What would I do if I were in this situation? This is Stanislavski's "magic if," and the operative word here is "I." The more concretely you can visualize your self in the character's position, the richer your ideas for physical actions in the scene will be. A major pitfall for actors doing cold readings is the tendency to waste time analyzing the scene, without settling upon something personal and specific to play onstage. "To be able to dissect a character in your mind," Stanislavski once remarked, "does not mean that you are a talented actor. There are many actors who can analyze their parts very well, but are unable to play them satisfactorily. . . . All you can do is to put the little word 'if' in the circle of your attention *with the help of your thoughts and your imagination* . . . and in this way begin to live with the images of your inner life."[5] Or again, more poetically: "With the aid of the circumstances set up by the playwright, magic 'ifs,' the actor opens out his wings of faith which carry him up into the realm of imagination he so sincerely believes in."[6]

There are no quick tricks to generating this belief in cold scenes such as handy "key word substitutions" discussed in chapter 4. The ability to believe is developed over years of training, and actors are supposed to have it in performance, like turning on a switch. Some coaches recommend a list of questions the actor should ask of the scene in order to stimulate imagination and help belief. Jane Alderman, for example, a Chicago casting agent and Goodman auditions coach, suggests the following: "Who am I? What am I doing? Where am I going? Who are we? What am I fighting for?"[7] Imagination and belief are especially necessary at a cold reading. You should rehearse on your own with new plays or other kinds of unfamiliar scene material—even with recipes or newspaper articles—in order to get used to quickly projecting yourself into the world of the play.

When you don't use some version of the "magic if," when you don't use your own rich life experience, then you're going to have to deal with intellectual analysis of the text. You'll be forced into using this dull secondhand knowledge instead of making unique choices about the scene. Directors seek this uniqueness in a cold reading probably because cold readings force actors to tap themselves at a moment's notice. As one director remarked, "The primary thing that I respond to in watching is do I sense a presence in the room that is unique, that is interesting, that is human . . . the more one is able to be there rather than the facsimile of presence."[8] Or again: "What you're trying to find out is, 'What are you really like as a person?' So you're usually telling them to read it simply. Very often I'll say, 'No acting. Just *say* this.' Look at the script, see what the words are, and then just talk it."[9]

Demand number three: remember that you can bring the play to life for the first time at auditions. No matter how tentatively directors may want to regard your audition they can't help but see each reading as a possible "play" onstage before them. And in many cases they don't know exactly what they want—it's up to you to show them. A director might already have done some conceptualization of the eventual production by the time he's ready to cast. Mediocre directors usually have done a lot of it and will have set opinions about how a scene or character should be played. They'll look for something specific at tryouts. But good directors leave themselves open to possibilities until the last moment—sometimes even until rehearsals are underway. And this is where a strong, confident audition, no matter how mistaken the interpretation, can pay off.

Although there are no standard criteria for evaluating auditionees, directors obviously consider two things when making a casting decision: how right a person seems for one or more of the roles, and the amount of potential he or she has that might be developed in a brief rehearsal period. The former is less important than the latter in a cold reading. To a certain extent these are interconnected. An actor who can pick up on the basic interpretation in a cold reading is demonstrating numerous acting skills and he may be coming very close to what the play calls for.

If you were asked to prepare a scene for callbacks the director would then be scrutinizing your suitability for the part very carefully. But in a cold first reading your appropriateness for any role is far less important than your ability to act: to establish strong and authentic relationships onstage and to play clear and solid actions.

Another way of saying this is to avoid at all costs shooting for the "correct" way to play a scene and try instead to bring something to life. The inhibiting fear of reading "incorrectly" is a common pitfall for young actors at cold readings, just as tension and mechanical performances are common traps with prepared monologues. Remember that the "meaning" of a play—no matter how well the production has been re-hearsed—will never be the same to every member of the audience. So don't worry about "meaning" in cold readings. Just play the material and "go for broke." An actor offers only images to an audience, not "meaning"; that's something for the writer or the spectator or the critic to discover. Just show the auditors that you can decide upon an action and play it clearly and strongly, and let them decide whether or not you can also play the action the director wants if he works with you in a month of rehearsals. Show potential.

You can't do anything about the director who's already made up his or her mind about a show: either you have what the director's looking for or you don't, and no amount of worry or second guessing is going to help you. But with a good director you can perform a vivid, strong cold reading and let the director know that he or she has an actor up there who is willing to play material with spirit and confidence.

To conclude, cold readings are often an unavoidable necessity in casting—in fact they may be the only kind of reading a director will hold. To do them well, keep these two methods in mind and make decisions:

1. What kind of play is it? What spirit infuses the scene?
2. What basic goals, needs, or dreams can your character have in the scene, and what concrete actions will express these needs?

Then remember what is going on at cold readings:

1. You're working under extreme pressure, so keep your choices and your playing simple and direct.

2. Use your personal experience; use your self in responding to the character's situation and to the choices he or she makes.
3. Bring something to life up there for the casting people.

Then *play* the scene.

Exploration 16: Cold readings for style

Using the scene from Hugh Nevill's *Love Rides the Rails* in the Appendix, rehearse a cold reading situation according to the following twelve steps.

1. Do not read the scene until you're prepared to time yourself.
2. Set a timer, or have someone time you, for no longer than ten minutes (the time you need should decrease to one minute as you become more proficient).
3. When time begins, take the scene and go off by yourself. Read the lines aloud. Ignore all stage directions.
4. Identify what happens in the scene (the psychological or situational events).
5. Identify what the character actually says (the sense of the lines).
6. Identify two different attitudes or points of view your character seems to hold towards the encounter with the other character (the manner or style in which the scene should be played).
7. Using the information from points 4 and 5 as baselines, read the scene aloud again, aiming to capture the *spirit* of the scene with one of the attitudes you chose to play in 6.
8. Read it aloud again, using the second possible attitude you picked out in point 6.
9. Quickly decide which of the possible attitudes plays better or feels more comfortable to you. You *must* choose one; don't waste time looking for a third possibility. This does not mean "feels safe" to you. It means something like "feels right" or "feels like more

fun to play" or "feels more appropriate in the context of the lines."

10. Read the scene aloud one more time in the manner you've chosen, trying to play it consistently according to the "spirit" that seems to govern the scene from beginning to end.

11. When time is called, perform your scene with your scene partner, who may or may not have prepared something on his own. As you practice with more scenes like this one be sure to work with both kinds of partners: an "unprepared" stumbling partner without much focus or approach as well as someone who is well focused and who thus forces you to react. You never know who your scene partner will be at a cold reading.

12. *Read this step only after you've performed the above steps.* If you've done the cold reading exercise correctly you should have come down hard on one of the following points of attack. Check yourself:

- *a potboiling soap opera* in which two characters' urgent need to prevent the train wreck overrides every other consideration
- *a wildly farcical* five minutes of desperate escape and incredible heroism, cornball love and drippy idealism, fumbling nervousness and ridiculous response to duty
- *an absurdly chaotic situation* in which people react like ping-pong balls to their own scattered thoughts and to the insistent demands of the outside world (all the while trying to maintain a sense of normality)

If your performance failed to convey any of these approaches, go back and read the scene again with one of them in mind. Explore the other one or two approaches also in order to learn more about the scene's potential. Although on paper each of the three above suggestions may seem very similar, you should find that in actual performance you are tending to stress different things as you do the scene in different ways. For example, in the first suggestion you may find yourself playing a strong sense of *urgency* as the action develops and that the physical business becomes an obstacle to actually running down the tracks to warn the train. In the second suggestion, you may find yourself yielding more fully to moments of sentimentality, to grim-jawed determination, and the like. Or with the third suggestion, you may find yourself registering moments of confusion, hesitating, and making snap decisions more than you would in either of the other two approaches. The scene will "play" well with any of the three approaches; what you are trying to accomplish is to discover which of the three feels best for you.

Remember that the more energetically you rehearse—the more commitment and absolute belief you bring to your approach—the more different each of the possible interpretations will become and the more vivid your acting will be. Follow up this exercise by rehearsing other unfamiliar scenes in the same manner. Keep at it until you get the hang of quickly settling upon a style you can play enjoyably onstage for five to six minutes. The trick, of course, is to *keep that point of view in mind as you perform each moment and to play it energetically.* Go for broke. If you're using this method correctly you should find that your performances are gradually becoming more lively and that concrete physical actions are taking care of themselves as you act. An important requirement of this exercise is that you learn to trust your own impulses about a scene and to go with your gut feelings.

Exploration 17: Cold readings for objectives and actions

Turn now to the scene in the Appendix between Louis XVI and the count in Paul Foster's *Tom Paine*. Each of these roles can be played by either sex, and this can lead to wildly hilarious line interpretations. Never mind about that —that's the audience's part. Your job is to find something specific to do, to go after and achieve in the scene. Follow these steps:

1. Set the time, agree on your character with your scene partner, take the script away, and read it aloud straight through.

2. Try to identify the events in the scene.
3. Try to identify the sense of the scene.
4. On the basis of this given information, try to identify what your character absolutely must have as a result of this particular encounter. This will probably be easier for you to do with the character of the count than with Louis XVI. Don't be afraid of speculating about an objective to drive your character. Be ready to go with your gut feeling.
5. Repeat the previous step, finding another objective.
6. Devise only three concrete physical actions you can perform in the scene that might express each of the objectives you just identified.
7. Read through the scene again keeping in mind *only one* of the possible intentions of your character. Increase your belief in the scene by visualizing concrete actions as you read. Then repeat this step using the second objective you decided upon.
8. Choose one of the two possibilities in point 7 which feels best to you. Reexamine your three physical actions to make sure they fulfill the objective. Then rehearse the scene one more time (if time allows) and head onstage.

Check yourself against the following possibilities for objectives and actions:

Louis XVI

- he wants to crush the English and to humiliate their king (he might squirm impatiently in his chair for awhile, speak in a brusque manner, and leap excitedly to his feet at the end of the scene)
- he wants to feel big and to be admired (he may pace languorously, study his body and clothes fastidiously, and gesture with exaggerated foppishness and much posturing)
- he is very bored and wants some fun (he may enjoy irritating the count by pooh-poohing, he may become preoccupied with some new court dance step during the con-

versation, and he may giggle childishly at the end when he sees how to play a nasty trick upon Beaumarchais)

Count

- he wants a shot at power and influence (his hands may be tense and restless, he may plant himself solidly and regard Louis with a steely look at times, he may eagerly introduce an idea but suddenly pull back when it takes hold in Louis' brain)
- he despises Louis but needs to con him into the plan (he may prowl around Louis like a cat, he may pretend to "improvise" the plan as he goes along, he may mock Louis to his face without Louis ever suspecting)

As you did in the previous Explorations, practice each of these objectives and actions until Paul Foster's scene becomes very different to you each time that you perform it. The trick again is to hold only one objective clearly in mind all the way through and to use only a few concrete actions to fulfill that objective.

Exploration 18: Advanced cold readings

As a final project for this chapter, the scene from David Mamet's *The Woods*, found in the Appendix, should now be rehearsed as a cold reading using either of the two methods we've just explored:

1. the style, point of view, or spirit infusing the scene
2. the objectives and concrete actions of the characters

No indication is given here whether the scene is best approached by one method or the other. The material is less obvious on its surface that Foster's *Tom Paine*. But the script is flexible in cold readings and can be successfully approached by either method: style or objectives. After practicing the material according to the steps in Explorations 16 and 17, you might find it helpful to look over some suggestions in the Appendix regarding the objectives and concrete physical actions that might work in the scene.

Callbacks

Working on material for callbacks is no different from working on your own scenes and monologues for a prepared audition. You should use the same methods—in a shorter time, of course—for preparations and rehearsals. The main difference is that you don't choose callback material. You choose only how you're going to play the material assigned to you.

Pay attention to rehearsing callback material strictly according to the director's suggestions. You may be told exactly what kind of a character is wanted. Or the director may want to test you further with a scene having special needs: witty repartee in the dialogue perhaps (*The Importance of Being Earnest*), or slinky and menacing body energy (Potemkin in *Celebration*), or the ability to discover everyday objects with spontaneity and marvel (*Kaspar*). That is what the director wants in the role, and if you don't supply it, you don't get the part.

So in general you rehearse for callbacks according to a certain interpretation you've been given. Within that, however, you must add the same kinds of unique choices you might have made in your own prepared material. How does the innocent but curious Cicely play the repartee with charming but "degenerate" Algernon at the top of act two? Where, when, and how does Potemkin move around Orphan during their first encounter in act one? And how does Kaspar "listen" to voices or handle his shoelace for the first time? You must make specific, concrete choices. This is Stanislavski's "magic if" working within the givens of the script and the director's wishes. So be sure that you add these personal choices to callback material. Don't try to be "correct"—be unique.

Many things happen at callbacks that are, of course, beyond your control. For example, in addition to looking at how close you can come to creating the kind of character wanted, the director will also be trying to "balance" the cast: to see how actors look and sound with each other in the given roles (which is always hard to determine at general readings). Is that potential leading man ten inches shorter than the leading lady? Then one may have to go. Are there some sparks flying when three or four actors are reading together, or does that particular combination of good actors just fall flat? Can you recreate that wonderful chemistry in character relationships that the director noticed at cold readings when you are on-stage at callbacks with another wonderful actor who read before you?

"The show" takes on a much more definite outline for the director at callbacks, as the pieces collected at general tryouts are fitted together to bring to life the world of the play. While you work on your own character, the one who was assigned to you, be aware that you'll have to adjust to the other actors you'll find yourself with at callbacks. Fit in, blend well, look to create an ensemble for the director. Listen and react to the other players in order to create the world of the play with the materials (literary and human) you have at hand.

Finally, a few minor rules concerning callbacks:

1. All material should be memorized.
2. Wear the same thing to callbacks as you wore to general tryouts if callbacks are the same day. If you have a day or two to prepare your callback, then wear something appropriate to the character.
3. Read the whole play.
4. Be prepared to explore new approaches to the material that the director may suggest during callbacks.
5. Come prepared for additional physical improvisations that the director may wish to conduct.

Chapter six

Musical Theatre

It's very unlikely that a young actor can go through school these days without getting a shot at a part in musical theatre: Broadway-style musical comedies, rock-musicals (*Celebration* and *Godspell*), operettas (*Brigadoon* or Gilbert and Sullivan), operas (traditional or modern, like *Threepenny Opera* and *Jesus Christ Superstar*), revues (*Oh, Coward!* and *Oh, What a Lovely War!*), or musical dramas (*Marat/Sade* and *1776*). Does the list sound complicated?

A musical show is just "a musical," right? Wrong. Musical theatre is the fastest changing, most experimental theatrical form in the United States. It is the most popular form of theatre—commercial and otherwise—in the United States. And if you think you can become a good (or even self-supporting) actor without doing a lot of musical theatre, you're dead wrong.

Shakespeare is music, song, and dance (among other things). So is classical Greek tragedy and comedy. Bertolt Brecht and Peter Weiss, the contemporary theatre's most radical (and most successful) political dramatists, wrote musical dramas, operas, revues, and the like to score their points. The Provisional Theatre, the San Francisco Mime Troupe, Chicago's Organic Theatre, and countless other producers and groups often include music-song-dance in their shows. In fact, *All That Jazz* and *A Chorus Line* are two musicals written about the competition for roles in musicals. Plenty of actors are hungry for it these days.

What is it about musical theatre that makes it so popular,

113

makes it the vehicle for flesh (*Oh, Calcutta!*), for sentiment (*The Fantasticks*), for the campy and macabre (*Sweeney Todd*), as well as for the ideas and insights of history's finest writers and thinkers? Well, the question is deceptive. "Musical theatre" is an academic phrase used to categorize plays for discussion and analysis and, like many academic terms, it has little to do with the real world. Lots of plays are being done that have substantial musical elements in them but we don't ordinarily refer to them as "musicals." And actors must perform them. The stage, up until the last century, has always included music in some form. Only in the past hundred years or so have we developed a body of plays, all of which studiously avoid the "theatricality" and song-dance-drama combination that musical drama implies—and which audiences throughout history have always flocked to see. Today the boundaries between "opera," "musical," "cabaret," and other forms are constantly breaking down, and actors need to be familiar with many musical styles.

It's probably the energy level that makes musical theatre so appealing. If you've ever done this kind of show, you know what I mean: you've really got to work. You must act, sing, and dance—often at the same time. The scenes and the emotions are somehow bigger than you find in straight plays. The stage action is faster, the encounters more intense, and the characters more cleanly developed. It's the kind of play that lots of people want to be in because it's fun. So much energy comes together in a musical show that the experience is bound to get you high: the sound of the orchestra, the cameo spots and flashy production numbers, the glitzy lights, costumes, and sets. One New York dramaturg has nailed down this principle very well: "The musical's arena is the outrageous, the wondrous, the screwball—life at its full rhythm—and more common than we think. As Martha Graham puts it, the creative problem is not to be larger than life, but as large."[1] Musical shows are total theatre, and that's one big reason why they're so much fun.

But don't forget that musical entertainment is also bread-and-butter for performers. I'd go as far as to say that more young actors are employed in musical shows each year than in all straight plays combined. This is especially true of summer stock, resort theatres, industrial shows, and "theme park" entertainments (Disneyland, Great America), which offer student actors the most accessible avenues to professional-level experience and paying work.

But musical shows, while ever in demand and always available, are also in many ways the most difficult challenges an actor can undertake, and they're tough to audition for. When you try out for a musical you'll have to convince directors that you're a "triple threat." You'll have to cut it as an actor, dancer, and singer. Michael Shurtleff reminds his professional students about auditioning for musicals that, "It needs everything an actor gives to drama and yet it needs more. More force, more economy, more relationship . . . more humor, more of everything an actor has to offer."[2]

Student actors usually have two problems when getting ready for musical auditions: either they regard this kind of a production as superficial and unserious or they feel self-conscious about singing and dancing well. The first problem is easier to deal with. If you share the viewpoint that musical plays are trivial, sentimental sops which boring people delight in spending money to see, then you haven't felt the power behind pieces like *Marat/Sade*, *Cloud Nine*, *Company*, or *Caucasian Chalk Circle*. And let's not forget that most of our most brilliant or popular living actors have performed on the musical stage at some point in their careers: George C. Scott, Gwen Verdon, Laurence Olivier, Julie Andrews, Roy Scheider, Richard Burton, and Christopher Reeve (to name just a few). The challenge is there, and you could do a lot worse than to follow their example.

The problem of talent, though, is a tougher nut to crack. It takes more than just desire to be able to sing or to dance. You'll need years of training to learn to sight read music or to develop a strong voice; and it takes years of sweat and physical workouts to pick up a choreography pattern or get the leg up for a two-hour performance. This is one area that needs attention early in your college career—not only for musical shows but for vocal power and expressive movement that you'll use in any kind of play you do. Plenty of actors pay to learn these skills later when they could have picked them up for far less cost while they were still in school.

Use your time wisely and apply yourself to developing song and dance abilities. A good theatre school will introduce you to these disciplines somewhere along in your program. Take a look at the following checklist to make sure you're heading in the right direction. In order to seriously compete for roles in musical shows, you'll need:

- the ability to sight read music
- the ability to carry a tune, both rhythmically and tonally
- the ability to sing with a clear, strong voice within a reasonable range
- the ability to project feeling, meaning, and belief into the lyrics
- the experience of discipline and form that comes from classical ballet
- the ability to create, improvise, and exploit your total physical resources that comes from modern and jazz dance
- familiarity with certain types of specialty dances such as tap, soft shoe, ballroom (including waltz)
- the experience of doing musical theatre, seeing musical productions, and listening to original cast recordings to get the feel for it

All of this sounds like work, and it is. Remember what I mentioned in the first chapter about pacing yourself and guarding against complacency in school. You know as well as I that you can do a minimum amount of work in many schools for four years and still graduate. If you do, though, you'll emerge woefully limited because you'll have developed a very narrow range of skills. And if you try to tackle the industry and get paid for your skills, the business will eat you up and spit you out very fast. There are just too many actors out there who have gotten the training because they've taken themselves seriously enough to work at it. As one professional coach explains it: "Many students come to New York with their M.F.A.s in hand, their glowing reviews in a portfolio, and their talents very sketchily developed through a too-casual acceptance of their (misleadingly) high campus status."[3] Take a cue from the song in *Company*, "and another hundred people just got off of the train." You want to be equipped when you get off the academic train.

Don't fall into the trap of thinking yourself "an actor" just because you can do a reasonably good job with a half-dozen characters in a more or less realistic way. That's basic, of course, and it might pass for TV trivia; but it isn't going to carry you for more than a few limited years—especially if you want to go on in the profession. Now let's take a closer look at the special features of musical theatre that you need to keep in mind as an actor.

Musicals and straight plays

The major difference between a musical and a straight play is rather obvious: you have to sing in musicals. A character must sing in musical theatre because there is absolutely no other way to express feelings. Song is a heightened form of human expression, similar to (but not the same as) poetry; and although it may seem unnatural to you at first and will tend to make you self-conscious at an audition, it really shouldn't. People sing all the time: they hum tunes to themselves as they ride expressways, they warble in their showers, they sing together in churches, at birthday parties, in saloons—people sing in all sorts of contexts in order to express what they feel. The impulse to sing is there; it's natural. So to act by means of song is no more unreal than to act in any other style.

The second thing to recognize is that music and dance are also parts of our everyday living: from muzak in the supermarket to your expensive stereo at home, from the Walkman cassette in your purse or pocket to the rock band you're going to hear tomorrow night. Because you're listening to music, your behavior and actions will change. This is the purpose of muzak, of course: you tend to buy products more easily. In movement terms, you may move closer to your date because you feel romantic, you may tap your fingers or toes, you'll tend to step to whatever beat your Walkman is pumping out—or you may even get right down to dancing in the beer hall when the band starts up.

Song and rhythmic movement are a big part of everyday

experience whether we take it in formal doses in a concert hall and ballet stage, or whether we're doing our own thing because it feels good to move and make sound. In a way, we've got to: we're feeling something that we've just got to let out and cut loose with in big or small ways. The same thing is true about characters in musical theatre. Words just will not suffice for them. Their songs and dances are lyrical extension of their feelings, their wants, their objectives.

This is how an auditionee should regard "style" in musical theatre. What the character needs to express is big, not "larger than life" but "as large," expressing what is "up to life." This is what Aaron Frankel and Michael Shurtleff mean when they say "more." The song or the music is not a pause in "the play" for a pretty tune or a flashy dance routine. It's an extension of the dramatic action and it flows from it. It adds zing to that action as it swells and overpowers, as it changes to lead into new actions, or as it connects one action to another—all the while that it drives across the apron to the farthest row of the balcony.

This magnification of experience is the essense of musical theatre and as an actor you must be up to the challenge. Your audition for a musical show must be strongly outer-directed. Never play dialogue or song just to the other character reading with you—play to the house also. There is no "fourth wall" when singing. As Shurtleff points out: "Each twosome scene in effect becomes a threesome, with the audience the third member of the scene."[4] The need to communicate with your listeners (discussed in chapter 4) means here that you must push beyond the stage to include them—often you present the scene or song directly to them. That's the way musicals are built to work.

There's no avoiding this if you want to do a good audition. All musical theatre looks for those moments, situations, encounters where it can turn out and embrace the public with urgency, surprise, and impact. Like Shakespeare's plays it is a vibrantly public theatrical form, and it is today's musical that comes the closest to creating the kind of theatre experience Shakespeare had in mind.[5] So don't regard this presentational quality of musical theatre acting as something artificial and unnatural; see it instead as a way of enlarging your character's feelings to their full, impassioned potential. As an actor you must want to share with the audience, whether it's a broad, fast-moving scene or a more intimate, deeply felt encounter. This need is built into the dramatic situations of musical dramas in a way that you will not find in straight plays, and you must play it at an audition.

This leads us to the second piece of advice about musical theatre auditioning: When you're given cold material at an audition realize that a scene is not likely to be self-contained or to have a climax in the words alone; rather the dialogue will often move toward the song as its dramatic peak. This is something that frequently confuses young actors, because they're far more word-oriented than song-and-dance or image oriented. You need to be familiar with the construction of dramatic action in musical scenes, part of which involves zeroing-in upon a few bold aspects of life that the play can explore in a lyrical, extended fashion.

A third point implied here is that events and character details—like dialogue—also tend to be compressed, economical, sketched-in and simplified in musical plays. Notice that I didn't say "simplistic" or "superficial" but only that the details you'll find in the script will tend to be minimal in comparison with straight plays. This is only logical when you stop to think about it. If a picture is worth a thousand words, then how many more words can be compressed into an exciting series of pictures or "images" presented in dance and music? In musical theatre, less is more. What you don't find in the script you must fill in by other means.

To a large extent, therefore, a major problem for the auditionee is to find ways of "filling in" the stage action at cold readings. Shurtleff suggests that you concentrate even harder than in straight plays upon creating a strong relationship with your scene partner. Other coaches I've talked with recommend close attention to the pace of your scene, working on the assumption that things should usually "develop" faster in musical shows because of the minimal events, dialogue and character details you need to work with. Still others insist that their students try not to "complicate" what is obviously a brief treatment, but focus instead upon whatever broad effects—in character, dialogue, or action—the scene may contain.

Certainly any of these approaches can be valuable to an

auditionee, and you should explore each to see just how valuable they may be for you:

- create a vivid relationship
- emphasize the fast-changing turns, discoveries, and changes in the action
- amplify dialogue, relationships, or events so you play the scene to its full potential

These three pointers are especially valuable for cold readings, but you should also keep them in mind when preparing scenes for callbacks. Use the same procedure outlined in chapter 4 for working-up material in straight plays, but remember these special problems as you proceed. To refresh your memory, these steps in preparation are:

- Select carefully and edit to retain just what you need
- Paraphrase to be sure of the meaning and motivation
- Identify goals and obstacles, and find concrete actions
- Divide your script into beats to give it shape
- Explore the vocal potential of the language
- Devise movement which reinforces the dramatic action
- Try to use the setting for mood, for urgency, or for belief
- Get some coaching or outside criticism you can rely on

Exploration 19: Musical theatre scenes

Look over the following scene between Polly and Tony from the musical *The Boy Friend*, book, lyrics, and music by Sandy Wilson. The scene contains no extraneous material, so there is no need for editing. (For callbacks, you do not edit the assigned material.) The pronunciation of certain words, though, is important for the playfulness of the style, so be sure that you consult a dictionary or language coach. One piece of stage business, dropping the box, is essential to mime, so you already have one "concrete action" to play. The diction is straightforward and contemporary, so you'll gain little from exploring the vocal sounds here. In other words, some of the steps in preparation can be eliminated or reduced because of the nature of the material.

Other steps, however, are crucial in order for the scene to work onstage at its full power and charm. For example, one way to "open out" the reading for the audience is to explore blocking patterns that frequently call for full frontal positions. In fact, the action suggests this by the shyness and embarrassment of the characters. They may "blush and turn away" at key points, sharing their nervousness with the audience and heightening the "charming mood" created by two young people falling in love almost at first sight.

Careful attention to other steps is also called for. Notice how the relationship can be established, how the few lines can be fleshed-out with mushy and tender sentiment, by playing the intentions and the obstacles strongly moment by moment. At different times Tony wishes "to bring" the package, "to praise" Polly, "to tell her" how much he'd like to go, etc. Similarly Polly wants "to meet" this cute young man, "to hide" her embarrassment, or "to date" him (along with many other objectives). The words may not give you much, but the scene can "fly" if you play these beats, colors, threads strongly and clearly.

The turns come quickly and the pace must not suffer even though the moments must be played fully, one-by-one!

Tony:	(*Coughing.*) Er—excusez-moi!
Polly:	(*Turning.*) Oh! You startled me!
Tony:	I'm sorry, miss. I'm afraid I came in the wrong way. This is the Villa Caprice, isn't it?
Polly:	Yes.
Tony:	I have a package here for Miss Polly Browne.
Polly:	Really? How funny!
Tony:	Funny? Why?
Polly:	Because I'm Polly Browne.
Tony:	Well, it's a very pretty name.
Polly:	Oh, thank you.
Tony:	And you live up to it.
Polly:	Oh!

Tony: I'm sorry, Miss. I'm afraid I'm forgetting myself.
           Here's your package. (*Tony hands Polly the package. Both*
           hold onto it. They are looking at each other. They both release
           it and Tony picks it up and gives it to Polly again.)
Polly: Oh, thank you.
Tony: If you don't mind my saying so, it's an awfully pretty
           dress.
Polly: Yes, it is, isn't it?
Tony: Yes, I'm sure that you—I mean it will be the prettiest
           at the Ball.
Polly: Oh, I don't expect so really.
Tony: I do. In fact I know it. I—
Polly: Yes?
Tony: Well, perhaps I'd better be going.
Polly: Oh yes. Oh no. Oh yes, perhaps you had. (*He turns*
           to go.) I say!
Tony: (*Turning back.*) Yes?
Polly: You're—you're English, aren't you?
Tony: Yes, as a matter of fact, I am.
Polly: You don't seem like a messenger boy somehow.
Tony: Don't I? Well, to tell you the truth I don't usually do
           this sort of thing, but just at the moment I'm afraid,
           I'm rather on my beam ends.
Polly: Oh, what a shame! And at Carnival Time too.
Tony: Yes, it is a pity, isn't it? I was hoping to be able to go
           to the Ball tonight. I'll be watching.
Polly: Will you?
Tony: (*Pause.*) Of course.
Polly: Why don't you come too?
Tony: Me? Come to the Ball?
Polly: Yes. Why not? I've got an extra ticket and—Oh dear,
           you must think me terribly forward.
Tony: No, I don't. I think you're terribly—
Polly: Yes?

After two or three rehearsals with your partner (remember to memorize scenes assigned for callbacks) you should feel pretty much on top of it. The next step is to continue rehearsing until you can perform the scene consistently the way you want it. Despite the apparent simplicity of the material, there are several key decisions—unique choices—which only you can make. At what point, for example, is

Tony actually captivated by her beauty: at first sight? When he learns her name? When the box drops? Perhaps all three—and then how do you build them onstage? Other questions might be asked of Polly. When does she get the impulse to ask him to the Ball (timing)? Where and how quickly does she start thinking of questions "to bring him back": when he starts to leave (pace and timing)? The scene has much potential. One final word of advice: Polly's last line leads directly into the love duet, "I Could Be Happy with You," which Tony begins, so don't play the last four to six lines as an ending; play them upbeat as a "launching."

Turn now to the scene between young Arthur and Guenevere from Lerner and Loewe's *Camelot* in the Appendix. This material is more complicated than that from *The Boy Friend* because of the greater emotional range and because each character has strong goals to play throughout the entire scene. Once again, pace is important: the emotions must be sincerely felt and expressed but there is a playful spirit in both characters—especially in Guenevere—that keeps the scene moving briskly along. Timing is critical, the mood stays buoyant, and beneath the surface charm of surprise and romance there is ample room for unique choices on the part of the performers. Why doesn't Arthur reveal to her that he's the king? And how does this "subtext" influence the actor's line deliveries and concrete actions? What makes Guenevere so curious about him, and how does the actress play this (a "unique choice" for her)? Does she really want to scrap the royal wedding that has been arranged? Or does she instead just want to find some momentary adventure on her way to the castle? How does the actress play this?

Two final clues about this scene. It begins right after Guenevere sings "Where are the Simple Joys of Maidenhood?" to herself (not knowing that Arthur is listening); and her final line leads directly into Arthur's famous song, the title song of the play, "Camelot." Practice the scene only after listening to these numbers on the original cast recording (not a popular song arrangement). This will help you get the feel of how music often controls the beginning and ending of scenes in musical theatre. The songs may also give you some ideas about character motivation during the scene.

Selecting the song

Probably the most difficult feature of musical theatre auditioning is the singing. For an actor song auditions are much
more terrifying than monologues or scenes simply because
they make you feel so "naked" onstage—nothing but your
voice to work with, nowhere to hide, and if you aren't a good
singer people will discover it right away. I know I always feel
this way at a singing audition—as though it were alien ter-
ritory. Speech, after all, is like conversation almost. But song
isn't. It's comforting to keep in mind that singing auditions
are a trying experience for most actors, amateurs and professionals, because they can't "fake it" or "wing it."

Generally speaking, most actors are not well trained as
singers, and the auditors are usually faced with a grim choice:
casting a strong actor who might have to fake part of the vocal
sections, or casting a fine singer who'll need some help struggling through the dramatic parts. Casting people are never
consistent about their preferences in this regard, and the problem arises frequently in collegiate and summer stock productions. Robert Peterson, a professional director who works
nationally with opera companies and lyric theatres, makes a
strong case for good singing abilities over the performer's
dramatic skills: "What I'm interested in seeing is do they have
enough power to carry the strong musical moments . . . do
they have a strong enough presence when they're singing.
There are actors who are really quite uncomfortable with singing, and when they get into those moments that are fairly
strong dramatically *and* musically, they either lose it or they
end up shouting it or speaking it."[7]

The type of show, of course, usually dictates the casting
needs. In the original production of *Company* in New York,
for example, Hal Prince (director and producer) worked in
the following manner: "Everyone in the company had to sing,
after a fashion; everyone had to dance, after a fashion. But
as they were to be real people, their footwork and voices were
subordinated to their performances. Which is not to say some
didn't sing well or move well. Some moved with agility, just
as some of your living-room friends move with agility, but
others were klutzes and we wanted that."[8] As a collegiate

actor, however, it's best not to bank on your future in the theatre as a klutz—even though the opportunity to perform as one may occasionally arise!

For young actors seeking roles in collegiate shows or entrance-level paying work in summer theatres, you need to concentrate upon performing the song dramatically instead of giving a song recital (with pear-shaped vowel sounds and studious attention to the composer's score). "Most of the people who are auditioning you—agents, casting directors, directors, choreographers, lyricists, librettists—are not as interested in the actual singing as in how you look, move, and fill the envisioned roles," remarks Jack Wann, an auditions coach and professional director from Kentucky. "The composer and the musical director are the only two people who are vitally interested in true vocal expertise. You must be able to act and perform with style to be hired to sing in most musical comedy companies."[9]

If you're an actor who is stronger in scenes than with songs, one way to market yourself successfully at an audition is by careful selection of material. In the few brief minutes that you're onstage you should have little trouble with about eight measures of a good song that will earn you a callback. Selecting and editing song material is no different from working on monologues: you don't have to do the whole song from the beginning. Edit your material so you get about eight bars of good lyrics for an exciting performance. You absolutely must work with a vocal coach. At the end of this chapter is a list of songs that are suitable for rehearsals and auditions. But before you begin selecting, editing, and rehearsing, here are a few basic things you should know.

The first requirement of a good audition song is that it be a show song and not a pop song, a folk number, a jazz melody, or something else. When I'm casting a musical show—whether it's operetta, cabaret, children's theatre, or Broadway score—I want to hear actors performing something that's written for the stage. I want something designed to push across the apron a situation, a character, or a relationship to a theatre audience in order to entertain them because that's what the actor will have to do in the production.

A show song will move and develop into something because it's made to be dramatic, theatrically exciting, and just plain "big." To return to Aaron Frankel again: "A show song is a heightened action springing from a dramatic context, and as a result reveals character, develops situation, forwards plot. It ends somewhere else from where it started, it makes a difference. A pop song has no such specific pressure and function. It is an entity unto itself, which does not go anywhere. . . . A pop song furthers moods, not actions."[10] Zero-in upon material specifically written for actors and you'll give yourself an edge. Good material can sell you.

Second, be aware that show songs—because they are "dramatic"—will develop, change, and turn direction vividly and frequently. In a cold singing audition, keep this in mind and play those turns with strong contrasts in your acting. Look to do this when preparing for assigned callbacks or when preparing two or three songs in full for general callbacks after the first initial tryouts. There will always be a climax in a show song, but you'll frequently find a twist, a surprise, a reverse at the climactic point as well. It may be "soft as well as big," the climax may be reached quickly or slowly, but the punch or payoff is always present in the show song. So look for that, and play it.

This doesn't necessarily mean that your song must be energetically paced, by any means. Some student actors are good with upbeat numbers while others feel at home with a gentle, lyrical piece. Most auditions and callbacks will require two contrasting selections (although you may have time to perform only one in general tryouts): a ballad or "legit" song (your actual singing range) and a "belt" or specialty number (something that shows other vocal strengths you may possess). The first is mandatory; the second is necessary to have on hand because at a general audition you are mainly concerned with showing the directors your vocal range and your ability to create belief in the song. Whether this is best accomplished by an exciting upbeat "belt" or a tenderly felt ballad is up to you and your coach to decide.

Some final points about selecting material that is appropriate for you at an audition: remain within the maximum time limit and choose songs that you feel comfortable with, ones that you can sing well. Avoid personality or signature songs that were written for a star performer. No song should be bigger than the actor who is singing it.[11] You will need to work up several songs, of course. At callbacks or at general collegiate-level tryouts, directors often ask to hear more of what you can do. You'll need at least four numbers, unless you're a very accomplished singer, in which case you should have a full repertoire on hand:

- Eight to sixteen measures for general auditions that will get you a callback
- A second eight to sixteen bars from a contrasting song, either for callbacks or for an auditor's request at the general audition
- Two complete songs ready to go if necessary (these might reveal any other strong points you may have or they might be chosen for the particular type of show being cast)

All four numbers should contrast strongly either in tempo, mood, vocal range, or special vocal technique; never repeat yourself (because you always have too much to offer).

Working up the song

Because of the highly specialized nature of singing (which does not ordinarily occupy a substantial part of the actor's training) this chapter will not attempt to lay out a thorough method for preparing show songs. That is something best left to your singing coach or to an intensive special workshop at the professional level.[12] Find a coach who works in musical theatre styles and not one who is primarily just a music or voice teacher. The reason for this, again, is because musical theatre performance and auditioning is radically different from vocal recitals. The only exception to this is auditions for operas and operettas, which require excellent voice technique (the auditions notice will usually indicate this). In all other cases—even if you are an accomplished singer—you need to work with a coach who understands what it means to sell a song to a theatre audience. Though I have cast young singers and seen a few hired for paying work in stock companies, their usefulness to the production and the theatre company is extremely limited. There just isn't enough time to work with them on acting skills, and they are always second choices when no suitable actors are available.

The three general steps in preparing show songs are roughly analagous to the separate stages of preparation for dramatic monologues: analyzing the lyric, clarifying subtext and motivation, and staging the piece. In fact, one valuable way of looking at an audition song is to regard it as a dramatic "soliloquy": it is presented by a solitary character directly to the audience, and it is a highly revealing, emotionally compelling theatrical convention. The major difference is that songs are much more personally revealing than soliloquies, because the human voice (a song's exclusive vehicle) carries an indelible stamp of the person behind it. It is one thing for the vocal director to say that your vocal pitch should be true, your breath support adequate, your tone and timbre pleasant, and so on, and it is quite another to cast a person because his or her voice belongs to a thrilling actor who is sensitive to the meaning of the lyrics, emotionally in touch with the subtext, and creating a wonderful presence and belief in the song.

Again, remember that you can't "hide behind" your character onstage, and this is especially true of singing auditions. Your performance will reveal you no matter what the content of the lyric may be. Your first attempt at auditioning is bound to be self-conscious and you simply must get used to this; remember that it's true of amateurs and professionals alike. Young actors are always more comfortable with handling singing technique than they are with expressing their personal selves through the song. In fact, the very first pitfall you'll encounter in performance is the trap of listening to yourself as you sing instead of wholly committing yourself to belief in the dramatic situation contained in the song. The only antidote for this is thorough preparation of your material. Stage fright or stage nerves are the necessary counterpart of good acting; they're the tension (not "tenseness") that makes for compelling dramatic performances. But only solid preparation will help you channel that nervous energy effectively. Begin your preparation by memorizing and then analyzing the lyrics. As with spoken monologues or scenes, first do a literal or "denotative" paraphrase of the lines, followed by a subtextual paraphrase that identifies underlying meanings or feelings (the latter is crucially important for song). Apply the who-what-where formula as you do this, answering important questions about the character singing, the dramatic situation, and the locale:

- What is the age of the character? His or her background, upbringing, educational experience, sex, social class? Is there anything else indicated either by the lyrics or by the show from which the song is taken that tells you about the character's identity? What is his or her personality like?
- What are the facts, the events of the lyric? What is the song "about"? Does it tell a story, make some appeal, or express some kind of need directly? Is it self-comment or questioning? What "problems" or "issues" do the lyrics deal with?
- What context surrounds the song? Who is listening and where is it being sung? Is the character reacting to "given circumstances" that have just occurred or are about to occur? What is special about the "where"? Why must the song be sung now (regardless of whether the lyrics describe a past, present, or future situation)? What circumstances can you find either in the lyrics themselves or in the context of the play which justify this character's song at this particular moment?

The answers to these questions should be fully written out. Once you've done this, construct your paraphrase either in the form of a prose monologue like that of *Same Time, Next Year* (Appendix) or like an "interlinear translation," an example of which follows. Notice how the interlinear model (preferable for songs) does not attempt to duplicate either the rhythmic patterns or the rhyme of the original lyrics. At this point you should be concerned only with what the song is actually telling us.[13] Musical values must be set aside for the moment so you can clearly see just what the words are saying.

"Won't You Charleston with Me?"[14]

1 Won't you Charleston with me?
  Would you like to dance "The Charleston" with me?

2 Won't you Charleston with me?
  Would you like to do "The Charleston" with me?

3 And while the band is playing that
  While the band is playing that

4 Old vodeodo,
  familiar rhythmic pattern

5 Around we'll go,
  We'll dance around the floor

6 Together we'll show them
  Together we'll show everyone watching

7 How the Charleston is done.
  How to really dance "The Charleston"

8 We'll surprise everyone
  They'll be surprised to see what fun it is

9 Just think what heaven it's going to be
  Just imagine how wonderful it will be

10 If you will Charleston, Charleston with me.
  for us to do "The Charleston" together.

I've purposely chosen a rather simple lyric to illustrate paraphrasing because it reveals how much essential information an actor can gain from an apparently uncomplicated song. For example, the choice of words ("diction") shows that the characters are fairly well educated and that they are aware of manners belonging to a certain social class (by comparison, the fragmented sentences and sexually blunt language of many punk rock popular songs also reveal characters, though of an entirely different type). The kind of dance mentioned stamps the song as belonging to a definite historical period; and the "voh-dee-oh-do" cliché suggests something about those characters' enjoyment of the dance itself (the rhythmic vocalizations and hand gestures of the Charleston that were the equivalent of our grunts, yells, and physical movements in modern disco styles).

Practice speaking your paraphrase aloud in a normal voice several times, delivering it in any physical manner or position you choose. You will also find it helpful to repeat movement improvisations numbers 1 and 5 in chapter 4 in order to explore staging possibilities and to avoid placing too much emphasis on just reciting the words.

The next step is to write a paraphrase of the lyric's connotative meanings, trying to capture:

- the spirit or essence of the words themselves
- the feelings of the characters who are singing
- your own particular associations ("substitutions") that help to make the song meaningful to you

Songs, just as any other artistic medium, can always be explained on at least two levels: the surface and the subtext. You've nailed down the literal meaning of the words; now just what do they really "mean," imply, or suggest to you and to your listener (the vis-á-vis)? What do you read into it? What will the audience get from it? The answers to these questions will take you much deeper into the song's purpose, the character's motivations and feelings, or the importance

which this dramatic moment holds than the lyrics can do by
themselves.

It is here in the connotative paraphrase that you will uncover the lyric's genuine power, its source of inspiration, that
gut feeling for which the words and music are only an awkward but necessary vehicle, maybe even "a mask." Observe
how one student discovered a paraphrase for the same
"Charleston" song which genuinely captures the character's
responses, intentions, and feelings:

> Hey Sal! Come on, baby—let's boogie! Take my hand and leave
> this dinner table behind. Let's get right down and boogie!
> What'chyou say! Push and pull and bump and grind and burn
> it out! Hey! Y'hear me talkin'? You are sooo fine—you turn me
> on with your foxy eyes and long legs and smiles and shifty
> moves! Shake that thing and get it on! Let's knock their sox off
> down on the dance floor. Turns, kicks, flips, and you name it!
> I wanna feel that beat and move it out like it's all happenin'
> right here and now! Stop hangin' back—grab on! Come on let's
> do it while the band is wailin'!

Notice how this student has specified his vis-á-vis, the
locale, and even some anatomical details concretely. There is
also evidence of personal "substitutions" both in names and
in diction. Above all, the paraphrase certainly captures the
feeling of excitement that the characters, Bobbie and Maisie,
must project in the song. Compare this paraphrase with the
way in which the song is sung on the original cast album.

The connotative meanings of songs are crucial in an actor's work because music does not work on its listeners in an
intellectual way—it works on feelings, emotional responses,
suggestive images that are beyond and beneath the level of
the word that is spoken or sung. Plays, too, work on audiences in a manner that is always irrational, sensuous, image
oriented—whether you're speaking of Sophocles, Shakespeare, Grotowski, Brecht, or any writer/director of compe-
tence. In the show song you see this principle wonderfully
put into action.

The task now is to take this source-energy found in the lyric's connotation and make it into a performance. The trick is to hold onto the connotative values while you gradually return to the lyrics, and then finally to the lyrics and music. Begin with movement improvisations 2, 3, and 4 in chapter 4. Try to hold the connotative paraphrase in mind as you move and your coach or a tape recorder delivers the lyrical line; gradually "come into sync" with the lyricist's words in rehearsal by whispering and then speaking. When you can finally speak the lyric at full volume, move freely and flexibly in tune with the connotative meanings as you do, and still retain all the charged-up energy that your subtextual paraphrase contains, you can begin to work with your rehearsal pianist.

This sequence of rehearsing a show song must be followed closely because once the pianist begins to add the music—either little by little as you rehearse or by setting down accompaniment on a cassette or tape—you will gradually begin to feel the connotations slipping away. The process is extremely difficult; but if you attempt to sing the lyrics without the underlying gut feelings and motivations you'll produce only dead vocalizing, the equivalent of "phoning-in" the performance. Expect to be awkward and off-base the first few times you try it. Even if you can hold onto the subtext for a few lines or phrases here and there as you sing, you'll be amazed at the difference in life, in energy, and in response that your singing then takes on.

Exploration 20: Musical theatre songs

Visit the public library or a record store and obtain an original cast recording of the musical *Company*. Get the sheet music to the song "Being Alive" from that show. Then put these items aside for the moment: do not listen to the recording or have a pianist play the music. Begin paraphrasing the lyrics, following the who-what-where method outlined above in preparing the Charleston number from *The Boyfriend*. The lyrics to work with are as follows:

"Being Alive"[15]

Someone to hold you too close,
Someone to hurt you too deep,
Someone to sit in your chair,
To ruin your sleep . . .

Someone to need you too much,
Someone to know you too well
Someone to pull you up short
And put you through hell . . .

Someone you have to let in.
Someone whose feelings you spare,
Someone who, like it or not, will want you to share
A little a lot . . .

Someone to crowd you with love,
Someone to force you to care,
Someone to make you come through
Who'll always be there, as frightened as you
Of being alive,
Being alive, being alive, being alive . . .

Somebody hold me too close,
Somebody hurt me too deep,
Somebody sit in my chair
And ruin my sleep and make me aware
Of being alive, being alive.

Somebody need me too much,
Somebody know me too well,
Somebody pull me up short
And put me through hell and give me support
For being alive, make me alive
Make me alive,

Make me confused, mock me with praise,
Let me be used, vary my days.
But alone is alone, not alive.

Somebody crowd me with love,
Somebody force me to care,
Somebody let me come through,
I'll always be there as frightened as you,
To help us survive
Being alive, being alive, being alive.

Make a cassette or tape recording of these lyrics, speaking them in a near-monotone without trying to add any emotional expression to your delivery. Then when you've completed both the literal and connotative paraphrases, rehearse them according to the methods in chapter 4. The next step is to play the show album and listen to the professional rendition of the song several times. Practice whispering or "lip synching" the lyrics (do not sing them or move to them) until the melody and phrasing are familiar. This should take about thirty minutes, after which you should return to your subtextual paraphrase and correct it. Be sure it contains all the meanings suggested by the singer's rendition as well as those associations that you formed while listening. Finally, rehearse the words of the song one or more times, speaking the lyrics and improvising movements and gestures spontaneously (do not set any blocking yet). When you can speak the lyric at full volume and still retain the connotative subtext much of the time, then you're ready to begin connecting the lyric to the melody line.

This basic rehearsal for show songs should be followed systematically; once you've done it properly you'll be able to rehearse other songs more quickly because you'll find your own best approaches—personal approaches—for working up material. You'll probably discover that working with a pianist this first time through is a difficult process; try to ask a friend to help out because it does require patience.

Have your pianist begin in small ways, playing only the single notes of the melody line, or (as David Craig suggests) playing only the belltones, the starting notes, for you to build your song up gradually. You may need to correct the phrasing in a few places in order to bring the sheet music into line with the album, or vice-versa. Later on, with pieces that you select by yourself, you'll have to work out with your pianist the phrasing and arrangement you desire and correct the sheet music accordingly. This is essential for auditioning because you must give the auditions accompanist a clear copy of the music that you want him or her to play for you. If you plan to audition with a prerecorded cassette as accompaniment, then your own pianist will be able to "set down a track" exactly the way you want it. In either case, keep in mind that you do not have to use the published arrangement in your final version (and never use the sound track from an album); use only that arrangement which helps you to perform the song best.

final points for song auditions

As I pointed out earlier, the preceding section does not represent an all-inclusive preparation for working up song material; it's only a basic method of approach that should be followed. You'll certainly want to modify it depending upon the needs of the particular song, your own strengths and weaknesses, and the preferences of your coach. What follows here are a few brief suggestions to keep in mind along the way.

1. For highly competitive and serious auditioning (paying work, scholarships, etc.) always bring your own accompanist.
2. If you plan to give sheet music to whomever happens to be playing at auditions, always give that person a clean, final copy and never ask him to rearrange or change something on the spot.
3. If you use a cassette for accompaniment, be certain that the tape is cued-up and the volume is preset loud enough to be heard, but not so loud that it distracts attention from you.

4. Cue the pianist or cassette operator with only a single small gesture from one hand or a simple nod of the head, then forget about it.
5. Never try to dance and sing simultaneously; dance auditions are always conducted separately.
6. Never sing to the auditors. The only thing that is worse than someone acting directly to you is having an auditionee sing at you.
7. Your strongest point of visual focus is the middle of the orchestra section (main floor) or slightly over the auditors' heads if you're on the same level. Begin the song with this point of focus, end with it, and return to it at all key places in the song.
8. Change your visual focus to left or right of center only when the lyrics (not the music) seem to call for it.
9. Keep your movements and gestures minimal. As with monologues, your blocking and gestures—like visual focus or "spotting"—should be motivated only by the lyrics, the thought pattern of the character who is singing.
10. Believe absolutely in what you are singing, "fill" each and every line completely before moving on to the next.

Sex	Type	Title	Show	Song Writer Composer
M-F	belt	"This Can't Be Love"	Boys from Syracuse	Rodgers and Hart
F	belt	"Matchmaker"	Fiddler on the Roof	Bock and Harnick
M	belt	"What a Day This Has Been"	Brigadoon	Lerner and Loewe
M	belt	"She Likes Basketball"	Promises, Promises	Bacharach and David
M	belt	"Kansas City"	Oklahoma	Rodgers and Hammerstein
M	ballad	"Colors of My Life"	Barnum	Coleman and Stewart
F	ballad	"Love Makes Such Fools of Us All"	Barnum	Coleman and Stewart
M	belt	"50 Million Years Ago"	Celebration	Schmidt and Jones
M-F	ballad	"Where or When"	Babes in Arms	Rodgers and Hart

Sex	Type	Title	Show	Song Writer Composer
M	ballad	"I've Grown Accustomed to Her Face"	*My Fair Lady*	Lerner and Loewe
M	belt	"Meeting the Wizard"	*The Wiz*	Charlie Small
F	ballad	"I Loved You Once in Silence"	*Camelot*	Lerner and Loewe
M	belt	"Sit Down You're Rocking the Boat"	*Guys and Dolls*	Frank Loesser
F	ballad	"Till There Was You"	*Music Man*	Meredith Wilson
F	ballad	"Send In the Clowns"	*Company*	Stephen Sondheim
F	belt	"I Cain't Say No"	*Oklahoma*	Rodgers and Hammerstein
F	ballad	"Soon It's Gonna Rain"	*Fantasticks*	Schmidt and Jones
M	belt	"Consider Yourself"	*Oliver!*	Lionel Bart
F	ballad	"So Little Time"	*Don't Bother Me, I Can't Cope*	Micki Grant
F	belt	"Don't Tell Mama"	*Cabaret*	Kander and Ebb
M	ballad	"Why Should I Wake Up?"	*Cabaret*	Kander and Ebb
F	ballad	"I've Got a Feeling I'm Falling"	*Ain't Misbehavin'*	Waller, Link, and Rose

Chapter seven

Supporting Material

No matter what profession you choose to enter you're bound to reach the point where your output no longer sells you and you need other methods in order to find more work. This probably happens far more often in the arts and entertainment industries than it does in other fields. The corporate executive or secretary may change jobs as often as every year or two, but actors find themselves "up against it" every time their show goes down. Unless a professional has the great good luck to belong to a resident company somewhere, he or she is bound to be handing out resumes and photos and bending the ears of anyone who will listen. Even in collegiate settings you'll have to fill out audition forms for each play you do; and of course each time you head into civic theatre work, paying jobs, scholarships, and grad schools, it's a whole new ballgame for you.

An important part of this process is your "supporting materials," things that accompany your actual performance (the raw material) in order to help you get the role or job you want. It comes in three forms: a resume that lays out on paper who and what you are, a photo that shows your key physical features, and an interview that reveals what kind of person you might be to work with. These can be either very informal or highly formal affairs. For example, I've often taken quickie Polaroid shots of auditionees for college musicals just to refresh my memory of people's faces at casting time. But when I give my own resume and pic to a summer rep director, you can bet that it's typeset and that the photo has cost me some bucks to obtain.

Generally speaking, the collegiate actor ought to know how to present himself on a typical auditions form for collegiate and civic theatre tryouts (you can also give a prepared resume to directors). He or she should also be able to quickly highlight his background in the form of a "verbal resume" when asked to do so by directors at an audition or in casual conversation. After four years the graduating senior should certainly have a good promotional photo as well as a formal resume for professional tryouts, grad school applications, and scholarship competitions. Obviously these are things one learns to do "along the way" during college; and if you get some paying work in summer theatres while you're still in school, you'll work with a coach to develop this material well before graduation. It's essential to be thinking early about this need to skillfully present yourself on paper and in interviews, no matter what profession you decide to enter.

You'll also find that writing yourself up on paper is a valuable exercise in self-understanding, as your journal exercises have already revealed. I mentioned in chapter 3 that one of the important spinoffs of auditioning for summer theatres is the sense of self-confidence and objectivity about your talents that comes from exposing yourself to hard-nosed employers and from packaging yourself as a saleable commodity for those acting markets. While in school you can get a strong headstart on preparing yourself for hitting any job market by keeping your eye on good resume writing and interviewing techniques. Let's take a look at what is actually involved.

The resume

There is one fundamental point you must always keep in mind about preparing your resume: it is the only thing the directors will have after you leave the stage. Everything about the resume follows from this: the materials you use, the format for laying it out, the content you choose to include, and the wording of the information—*everything* should be geared to leaving the directors with a document that can sell you like an agent when you're no longer there to do it yourself.

Let's begin with the broad picture: the materials. Are you considering a clean white heavy-grade onionskin or parchment paper? That's good for starters. The parchment texture has a classy appearance and heavy-grade paper will stand up under much handling (as well as holding a photo stapled to its back side). As for the printing, instead of an ordinary typewriter, why not use one with italics or modern IBM or something equally distinctive? One of the machines in your theatre department office might be available to you for this.

But you can easily do better with only a little extra effort. Avoid the typewriter and have your resume printed. One West Coast director (who is also a graphics artist) points out: "A well set-up resume is extremely important, especially for paying work. Spend a few bucks to get a good clean bunch of vitas typeset and printed. You know much about a person from the visual format of their vita."[1] When you're preparing to audition for paid summer work, go to a quickprint shop for the minimum copies (don't print more because you'll need to update it periodically). Or take your resume to your school newspaper where they can typeset the master for very little cost. This will produce a document that communicates professionalism and dependability and that will certainly stand out from the rest in the director's hands. Give yourself a little edge.

Of equal importance is the format of your resume—the layout of the information. There are several considerations involved here. One is quick readability by people who don't have time to waste. As Gordon Hunt recommends in his book on professional auditioning, "The best resumes are designed so that a quick look will give us an impression of a performer's background and experience. . . . We want to be able to glance at a picture and resume, then put them either in the call or don't call pile. If the resume is not quickly legible, we often don't have the time to glean all the pearls from it."[2]

A one-page resume is absolutely essential for an actor. Although you may feel that you haven't enough experience to fill even one page, when it comes time to write it up you'll probably discover that you'll need to be selective—even ruthless—about the information you include and exclude. If nothing else, writing up a resume will force you to take a look at your college training and stage experience in an organized way, and you'll be surprised what it can add up to when it's staring at you from the printed page. No matter how mundane it may seem to you, your collegiate training tells directors that you're studying (many auditionees aren't) and that what you've listed on the page is somehow important to you. Whether or not you're a "working actor" isn't as important as the fact that you're "working at it" by attending classes.

In addition to confining your experience to one page, you also need to put up front what is most important to you. For example, in the section that lists your stage experience, put down first the roles that were your favorites, the ones that seemed "closet to home" for you. When listing your training, think about which classes and teachers were the most exciting. In the training and special skills section, list what things you do best, what skills you would like to do for the show or the producing group. Disregard chronology if you have to (listing in order of the most recent) and focus instead on what speaks best for you by getting that at the top of the list. You'll know it'll be read there.

Two final points about these listings: be sure they're current and honest. Don't try to save typing time or printing expense by writing in or tacking on your latest stage role at the bottom. Type the whole thing afresh each time you update it. And don't lie—it really doesn't pay. If nothing else, you'll probably feel so guilty about it that you won't be able to concentrate on much else during your performance or your interview. If you put down that you can tap dance be prepared to do it, and if you list a stage role, then be prepared to talk intelligently about playing it. Stand behind your resume and make it a true, solid reflection of yourself.

Examine the typical format for an actor's resume in the Appendix. There are six separate categories of information: name and competency; address; personal data; stage experience; training; and special talents. The only other categories you may add to this format are TV, film, and radio experience, if you've done any performing in these media at your college or elsewhere. The categories should be listed in the sequence above.

Your name (as you would want it to appear on all papers) should go at the top center of the page with the competency (actor-technician) on the next line below it. This is sometimes called the "designator" because it tells plainly who you are and what job you're seeking. An actor-tech means that you can act and crew shows; this designation must appear with your name at the top of the sheet for speedy reference by the casting people.

Your address is the next most important item, and it's usually placed on the left of the page. List your current mailing address and two telephones—one of which will always be able to take a message and know how to reach you within an hour or two. This is extremely important. Many summer producers, for example, will wait until the last minute before casting, and then they want speedy answers for hiring and contracts. The same holds true for any director who doesn't already know you—he or she will want to reach you quickly if there is something important to cast. You'd be surprised how many actors have lost roles simply because they were unreachable at casting time. *Always keep this information updated.*

Directly opposite your address goes personal information that should include only hair and eye color, height and weight, singing range, and age range. All this information is straightforward except for the last. "Age range" does not mean how old you are; it means what "physical type" you are. You may be twenty-two and look sixteen, or vice-versa. It's how you look that counts. Forget the kinds of roles you'd like to play or what wonders costume and makeup can do for you—just what do you look like if you were a "character" in someone's play—a juvenile (ten to sixteen), ingenue (seventeen to nineteen), romantic lead (twenty to thirty)? Let the director decide whether he or she can add or subtract years from your face and body; you put down the age range that you appear to be. Your coach can help you with this point.

The next category, your acting experience, can be laid out in different ways, but the essential information includes the name of the production, the role you played, and the producing organization—usually listed straight across the page. The information you include in this section will in most cases be the roles that you've played in collegiate productions.

Don't list things you did in high school, and don't waste space by including dates.

In addition to plays you might also wish to include roles you performed in acting classes if you did scenes as part of your studio work. Be certain, of course, that these are roles which you honestly feel you could play if cast in the part. This last point is very important. At times your teachers might assign things like Willy Loman in *Death of a Salesman* or Martha in *Virginia Woolf* just for the sake of practicing on a major part. But these would never be within the age range of young actors and shouldn't be included on a resume. If you've spent time working up a character for an acting class—writing a character background and analysis, researching the period, exploring play and scene structure and the language, rehearsing and performing a few scenes—then this is definitely the kind of thing to put down so long as you feel you could do a good job with the part in an actual performance. You may find that you understand better or can talk more enthusiastically about characters you played in this context than those you actually played in a production. When listing them, include the word "studio" after the name of your school. As your stage experience grows, of course, you'll need to drop these studio roles, replacing them with characters you played in actual shows.

Some students benefit from attending universities that have film and media departments on the campus. In fact, when looking for a college this should be a major factor in your decision for two reasons: these media offer actors the greatest opportunity for paying work, and you may find that your career plans change after a couple of years. Instead of remaining a theatre major you may choose to enter a media program. These days the crossover between stage, screen, TV, and radio/recording work is common among actors, directors, designers, and tech people. You would do well to have some media experience under your belt before you graduate.

If you have such experience, it's best to have another category on your resume to include this—don't lump it in with the stage roles. After the section headed "Stage Experience," include a separate section headed "Film and Television" or "Film and Media" (if you've done radio work in classes or campus radio stations). This may seem extraneous if you are auditioning for a part in a play, right? Well, yes and no. Obviously your stage experience counts the most (just as it does in the film and TV industry); but whenever I look at a resume that includes media work I'm impressed for two reasons. I can see that this person is seriously looking to broaden his or her background by media experience (and you're going to learn a lot just by doing this), and I may have a need for an actor who knows microphone or camera technique. As a summer rep director and actor, for example, I was often called on to do promotional things for our company with local radio and TV stations. So put it down if you've got the experience. It can give you an edge.

Two final points about listing your experience. First, word carefully your description of the producing group where you played the parts. If your school's theatre has a name under which the drama program operates, then use that name instead of the name of your school, which might be relatively unknown. "Pioneer Theatre Lab, St. Louis" reads better to a summer producer than "St. Louis Junior College" and "The Alternative Theatre, Seattle" sounds better than "Seattle Community Players." As for media listings, keep your descriptions as concise as possible. "Cal Berkeley Extension Films" or "WZKO-TV Milwaukee" or "Florida U. Grad. Film Dept." are all that you need. If a director wants more information, he or she will ask. Save space and avoid cluttering the page.

Second, if you've performed in a show with a guest artist be sure to say so in the listing. This happens in certain schools and very frequently in summer theatres, many of which import a "star" or two in order to draw audiences. A typical listing of this sort would read:

"Major Barbara" . . . Jenny . . . Indianapolis Summer Rep (with Suzanne Somers)

The final category on your resume is "Training and Special Skills." Again, keep your description as concise as possible for quick readability. Summarize your school work by men-tioning only how many years you've been studying what and where. Again, if you've worked under guest artists or teachers at your college, put down their names; it isn't necessary to describe what you actually did in the class or workshop. As the sample resume shows, you want to lead off with the type of skill you learned: acting, combatives, modern dance, gymnastics, singing, and so on, followed by the length of time you spent at it and where (or with whom). A few exceptions to this might be dialects (indicate your fluency in different languages) or music (which instruments you can play). Remember that "special skills" doesn't mean hobbies; as a rule of thumb, include only those activities that you could do in performance, activities that people might be willing to pay money to see.

Though it may seem to you unfair and inhuman to base part of a casting decision (especially for paying work) upon a resume that is a sketchy outline of your capabilities, you have no choice in the matter—and neither have producers. There is absolutely no way anyone can know your true potential short of actually seeing you play the part (which is patently impossible). Producers will judge your suitability in several ways: your audition performance, your resume, a conversation or interview with you, perhaps by contacting a director who's worked with you, or possibly by having seen you in some other show (in that order of importance). All this adds up to an "educated guess" about your talent.

With all these factors and especially with the resume, the trick to success lies in anticipating the "buyer's needs." This principle is every bit as true for theatrical resumes as it is in the business and professional worlds. It affects the kind of material you select for an audition piece, the role you choose to list under stage experience, and the questions you ask when it comes to talking with directors about yourself and the upcoming production. Place yourself in their shoes by recalling what it is they're looking for and how you can fit into that picture.

Do not misrepresent yourself in order to make yourself acceptable to their needs. At all times be yourself; but think of how your abilities and interests might coincide with the project at hand. No director wants an actor whose only identity is somebody else's expectations. You're not exactly a prostitute in this business, and you should not be willing to do *anything* to get the role. But you can adapt and adjust to the needs of the director and the play. You can do this best by bringing your unique qualities to the project.

If you don't get the part then remember it's not a personal rejection, it's simply a professional one. Nothing is ever personal in this business. You are who you are, and if a particular director can't use you, there's another one who will. Ruth Schudson, an equity stage and film actor with the Milwaukee Chamber Theatre and Milwaukee Rep, states this advice clearly for young actors: "Auditions are always rough; they get easier. Just don't try to impress anyone. Just go there and do what you know you can do, as honestly as you can do it. And whatever quality they're looking for may not be the quality you might show at that moment. It's not a personal thing. It's just that the director wants an element which he didn't see in you in that moment, and you have to remember that."[3]

Photographs

You'll need a promotional photo of yourself when auditioning for paying work. Most summer stock and dinner theatres require it. If your school is located in a big city where media work is done, then you might need a picture for work in commercials or as an "extra." It's always a good idea, too, to submit a picture to civic theatre directors who may not know you, and it's certainly a convenience for university directors who are auditioning large cast shows.

In general, if you're serious about acting as a profession, you'll want to have a photo stapled to the back of your resume at all times because you never know when you'll need it to slip into someone's hands. One of your college director's friends who produces in summer stock might come to see your school play; at the cast party, make it a point to meet this producer and slip him or her a resume. It might get you a phone call. When going backstage to congratulate your sister or a friend who did a walk-on with a theatre group in a big city, take your resume and pic with you in case you meet some directors. They might need stagehands, other walk-ons, or rehearsal assistants sometime and give you a call. Professional actors are never without these materials for slipping under doors, handing to people waiting for elevators or in rest rooms or in airport ticket lines. In the entertainment business, the resume and pic is the equivalent of a business card. They're very important, and they're "throwaway" items.

Photographs are simple problems to deal with; the only difficulty is that they cost money. There's only one standard format for pics: a glossy 8 x 10 inch black-and-white headshot. This gives directors an "honest" look at you, and it's relatively easy to reproduce. Photo labs have special equipment for duplicating these items in batches of twenty-five to fifty, which is what you'll need when you make the rounds of summer auditions. If you have the occasion to give anyone a formal resume, it's probably also an occasion for having the photo stapled to the back. You bring a resume and pic to general auditions for the directors, and you give them to the directors again at callback readings and interviews (you'd be surprised how directors happen to "lose" things in the shuffle).

The biggest problem you'll run into with promotional photos is that of finding the right photographer to work with. Needless to say, not just anyone who has the equipment, can use a camera, and can work in the darkroom will suffice. Many camera people, of course, will tell you they can give you what you need, but few will know anything about a promotional photo. Most photographers, especially young ones, will regard portrait work either as artistically unexciting or as "a piece of cake." But a professional knows that portraiture is one of the most difficult photographic assignments and that the good portrait artist is hard to find.

What this means for you is that you should expect to have to lead your camera person by the nose if you want to get what you need, and there are two places for you to begin. First, look through old photos of yourself and try to identify expressions, moments, and attitudes that you feel do you credit. These should be snapshot kinds of things and not character shots or show photos of you in a role. Directors use pics only to see what your face looks like; they want to know your basic features. So begin by taking an inventory of your facial expressions and deciding what you want to represent you. Don't assume that the snapshots you have on hand "cover" you completely. Spend time in front of a mirror when deciding what expressions and attitudes reveal you honestly, but "at your best." Perhaps your acting teacher or the school photography instructor can help with this.

Second, visit the library and look through theatre books and entertainment magazines for "press release" photos like the ones you need. Bring these samples with you so the photographer can see exactly what you're after. You must make sure the cameraman understands that you're after a "straight" promotional portrait for commercial purposes. You don't want an "artsy" shot of yourself, so ignore any of the photographer's suggestions for creating dramatic light and shadow effects, using color reversals, cute backgrounds, or exotic makeup. The pic should be an "honest you," flattering but pleasant and true in its basic approach, which will represent you after you've left the audition or interview.

For beginning actors I always recommend several basic procedures to follow when obtaining photos. If you continue with acting as a profession you'll learn more about photography and how to make it work for you. But in order to cover all the bases the first time around, keep you mind on the following guidelines:

1. The overall goal of your photograph is to "get you in the door." Directors see hundreds of pics, and look at each for only a second or two. Your photo therefore should arrest the director's attention and make a lasting impression. It won't get you the job, but it might get you a callback or interview.
2. Practice making-up before arriving for the photo session. Basic street makeup is required; you should need no more than four colors to mix and some transparent powder. Lighting and lensing will tend to distort certain aspects of your face (such as flattening the nose, making the lips pale, etc.). So create something flat-

tering that brings out your basic features without over-
doing or overglamorizing your appearance. Your hair
should frame your face and seem "natural" (though
better than "everyday").

3. Bring some music or a radio to the shooting session
which will help you to relax and feel in a good mood.
Don't hesitate to run though certain poses and expressions in order to warm up and to show the camera
person.

4. When looking over the photographer's prints for final
selection, be sure that the portrait has some life to it,
that the eyes are vivid and not lifeless, and that your
image conveys strong presence. As a general rule,
when you look over a sample of the photographer's
work, be certain that the portraits display his or her
ability to capture life instead of producing a mugshot
or a driver's license snapshot.

5. Get your contract terms clear in advance so that you
both know what you're paying for: number and size
of prints, ownership of negatives, fee, cost of additional prints, the amount of film to be used, and delivery time.

In addition to the 8 x 10 inch standard glossy headshot,
you may also wish to consider a sheet of "composites" for
your portfolio. A composite is an 8 x 10 inch color or black-
and-white sheet containing four to five small photos of an
actor in character poses of one kind or another. They may be
production photos or shots in costume and makeup specially
set up for promotional purposes. You use them only in interviews to show directors your range of parts—much like
other audition pieces you have on hand for callbacks in case
directors want to see "what else you can do." One technical
point about composites: since they're much smaller than a
single large headshot, make sure the subject is clearly visible
and that only the part of the character pose that is absolutely
vital is in the frame.

Photos cost money, of course. Like any other professional
you're going to have to invest more than just time and energy
in order to get the role or the paying work you're seeking.

Even a bankteller shells out for lunches, commuting, and clothes just as you'll have to pay for application fees, xeroxing, travel costs, resume printing, and photos. It's all tax deductible (if you need to think about that),[4] but there are cheap ways of going about it—especially if you're in college.

Your best bet is to contact the school newspaper, which usually has student photographers on its staff who do photojournalism assignments. Often the sports photographer is good because he's usually unafraid of movement and knows when to capture the moving subject. For the cost of a roll of film, chemicals, printing paper, and some "labor" you can usually get a good 8 x 10 print and negative. Take the negative to a photo lab (or send it to a lab in a major city) to have copies mass produced. Sometimes the lab will also put your name at the bottom or on the back for no extra cost—added insurance in case the pic gets separated from the resume.

Another possibility is the photography class at your school.[5] The instructor might welcome you as a good project because portrait work is a high-paying commercial field for his students to practice. In this situation you might even get to pick your final portrait from a wide variety of class assignments. Again, the negative is usually all you'll need to take to the lab.

Finally, if you live in a city large enough, you can pay a pro to do your photos. This is obviously the best—though the most expensive—way of going about it. In major cities, like Chicago, New York, Los Angeles, and San Francisco, there are photographers set up to do this sort of work. For a nominal amount, you can get fifty copies of a publicity photo that are expertly finished and perhaps even some composites thrown in. Professionals also give you expert advice on makeup and attitudes. The working actor always relies on pros to do this work because the photo—like everything else in the audition—must be as slick as possible to show the actor at his or her best and to communicate professionalism.

The interview-callback

Most interview situations that you'll encounter as a collegiate actor will be brief, casual affairs. In fact, the word *interview* has a formal sound to it that is probably more appropriate to the business and professional worlds than to university theatre programs or summer stock productions. The reason for this is that theatres are usually seeking people for short-time "employment"; most of the skills or "basic differentia" for the job are fairly evident from your audition performance. Qualities such as leadership, cognitive learning ability, grades, problem-solving skills, and written communication skills are inapplicable when it comes to casting plays.

Two things, though, are essential for proper casting and producers can learn about them only through an interview. The first is an indication of the total range of an actor's talent; and the second is an indication of an actor's ability to work with others and contribute to the ensemble feeling of the company. To phrase these goals from an auditionee's standpoint, this means that during an interview you should keep your focus on:

1. What skills the director is looking for, and either show or tell specifically how you can do or how you have done those things.
2. Expressing interest in and obtaining information about the different people connected with the play or theatre company.
3. Listening well to everything the directors explain or ask, and either performing just what they want or answering them as concretely as possible.
4. Maintaining a pleasant, cheerful, and helpful attitude.

For the most part, theatre interviews rarely consist of simple conversation; the interview will usually be combined with callbacks. In order to reduce the tension of the situation for everyone, directors will normally begin with some casual conversation before asking you to perform what they're interested in seeing. The only exception to this procedure might occur in an audition for small media work where the casting director needs to take a look at you as a "type." In this case a first "interview" will normally precede the reading, and if you're not the right type to begin with there won't be any need to have you actually perform.

Before discussing specific procedures to follow for an interview-callback, you need to recognize that these things (just like auditions) can occur anywhere and assume many different forms. When I was a collegiate performer, especially as a grad student, I told producers and directors about myself in offices, rehearsal halls, hot tubs, airline seats, bars, lobbies, cast parties (very common), and other places. "Interviews" can be totally unexpected off-the-cuff chit-chat or carefully set-up formal affairs. You might find yourself talking over pastrami sandwiches in a crowded deli, or while getting a tour of the theatre by a busy director—just as easily as you might be sitting in a classroom or office.

The goals of these situations vary too. Collegiate directors may not "interview" you at all because they haven't much to say or to question you about; they might have you do further readings or improvs, then proceed with casting. You're just another student actor up for a role, and they might already know you from classes you've taken. Summer rep and stock directors, though, might feel they can use your skills just from watching your general audition. When they call you back they may really want to talk to you about adjusting to their production schedule or to find out what else you can do in box office or management or to see if you're a dependable worker. You never know what you're in for. An interview-callback might be to apologize for not giving you one role and to ask if you'd accept another, or it might be an offer of a summer actor-tech contract right there on the spot. You should be prepared to pick up on anything. This is why the interview-callback requires maximum flexibility. ·

There are four guidelines to follow when approaching an interview-callback:

1. Prepare in advance by gaining all possible information.
2. Provide and obtain all the specific information about the role and/or job.
3. Practice good interpersonal communication skills.
4. Do a post-mortem on your performance.

Let's look at each of these in detail.

The first guideline, "gaining information," refers both to

your own situation and to that of the directors or producers. In the case of your school play, this means reading the play in advance, deciding what kind of role you want or how much time and energy you intend to put out, and what (if anything) the director is specifically seeking at callbacks. For a civic theatre callback you might also try to learn as much as possible about the nature of the group and the tastes of the director. For paying summer theatres you'd also have to decide before meeting the producers how much money you need to live on, what dates you'll be free to work, and how much money you'd be willing to accept.

All this information prepares you better for what might be coming, and much of it probably seems like common sense: reading the play beforehand, psyching-out ("second-guessing") the directors, and so on. But when it comes to serious paying work, student actors need to be careful. There are good and bad summer companies, and the bad ones can really be the pits. Prepare carefully by scouting-out as much information as possible, because signing on for a season with a raunchy company can be a worse experience than not being hired at all.

How do you find out what you need to know? Ask questions of your teachers, other actors at the auditions, or community theatre people, if you know anyone. Perhaps the theatre reviewer at your local newspaper might know something about the background of a particular company. Your best sources of information are either people who've acted in the theatre before or people who've worked with the group in some capacity. You need to know the following things about a summer company: (1) the basic working, living, and rehearsal conditions; (2) the kind of money involved and whether you can depend on being paid; (3) the working relationships between the acting company and the staff; and (4) the kind of talent in the acting company.

The second guideline about the interview-callback is to learn specific information about the position and the work required. Sometimes this is posted. Collegiate directors occasionally list roles "under consideration" when they announce callbacks; but more often than not you won't learn of your actual role (if you're cast) until the final notice is posted.

The same procedure is usually followed by civic theatre directors. In each case it's always to your advantage to engage the directors in conversation and give them more information about yourself. Make yourself known as much as possible (and always be tactful, not pushy about this) in order to give them more than just a good callback reading.

Because some callback-interviews often consist of nothing more than a further demonstration of your acting skills, you should ask questions in order for the directors to know you better. What roles are you up for? What does the director want from an actor in those parts? Can you stick around to watch or maybe to read again after your own reading? Be tactful and try to make your presence and your interest felt. Make yourself someone more than just another callback hopeful and you'll give yourself an edge.

With summer theatres you need to be much more aggressive, outgoing, and specific about the position. Interviews with these producers—while brief—are almost always more personal affairs and permit more questioning and answering. Learn about the theatre group by encouraging the director to talk about the show. What roles are being cast? Which ones are you up for? What does he or she plan to do with the production? What kind of audiences are expected?

Don't be surprised if the producer doesn't have a specific part for you right away. Many summer groups first hire a company and then do the final casting when the whole company assembles early in the season. If the position involves acting-tech, then be sure to find out what "tech" involves and mention where you'd like to help out: building sets, running box office, publicity, stage managing, or whatever.

You'll usually find that summer theatre producers will want to learn about you as a person, whether you'd be a good addition to their company. They are not just casting roles. Many actors can do a given role. Producers know that the ensemble will have to work closely together for about three months and that good working relationships are essential for a successful season. Be sure to give the producers some time to learn about your personality, and try to learn as much as possible about them too. No subject of conversation that they want to talk about is unimportant. Actors get hired because they're liked as people much more often than simply on the basis of their auditions. So during the interview keep asking yourself, Are these the kind of people I want to work with for a whole summer? What can I offer these producers for their production season? What kind of a summer theatre are these directors likely to operate?

Guideline number three, good interpersonal communication skills, is one that you must develop over time. They come from experience with interview situations and in one-to-one conversations. The basis of good one-to-one conversation is relaxation. Tenseness registers very quickly in a person's body-language, communicating itself to the listener and creating a climate of awkwardness. It also restricts the flow of your ideas, creating further embarrassment and blocking conversation. A few basic things that will improve your performance can be practiced beforehand and kept in mind during the interview-callback.

The first and most important feature of good interpersonal communication is listening well. While the director is speaking listen carefully and accurately; give yourself time to respond or explain, keeping in mind what the other person wants to know. Avoid rushing the interview-callback conversation, just as you avoid rushing the delivery of your audition speech. Phrase your answers and speak in a firm, alive, and vibrant voice (as much as the knots tightening in your stomach will permit). One hand rule to keep in mind applies to dramatic scenes as well as one-to-one conversations of this kind: listen, then respond.

A second feature of good interpersonal communication is maintaining open, outgoing, and alert nonverbal body-language. There is no universal agreement among speech specialists about what exactly goes into this, but some common pointers can be stressed here. Sit comfortably leaning slightly forward. This basic position says "alertness and eagerness." Avoid nervous, jerky movements with your hands; don't fidget. Keep your arms and hands loose so that you can gesture freely, and just as in acting, make your gestures controlled and complete. Harold Baldridge, director of New York's Neighborhood Playhouse and a long-time stage director, made this wry observation about actors' body-language during interview-callbacks:

Well, it's funny, you know, in different parts of the country, how actors come across in casting interviews. For instance, in New York where they're hungry and eager to work, they sit on the edge of their chair listening like this [he demonstrates]. And they ask what kind of a role they might do in my show. In the regional theatres—Chicago, say—they're a little more poised, more erect when you're talking, and they take more time to consider [he demonstrates]. And then they say something like, "That sounds fine. Now just what exactly did you have in mind?" But talking with actors out on the West Coast is completely different. They usually drape themselves over the chair and hook their thumbs in their pants [he demonstrates]. And they give you one of those sly kind of stares—very laid-back, you know. And it says to me something along the lines of, "So what can you do for me?"[6]

When and if you get to the income level of Al Pacino or Gretchen Cryer, you might also hook your thumbs in your Levis and be more selective about contract terms, But as a young actor you'd do far better to approach a director with an attitude that says, "How can I fit into your project?" Producer Michael Stuart, who auditioned nearly four hundred young women (eventually choosing two) for his off-Broadway production of *Nine*, complained of laid-back actors in the following terms: "What's with these people? Gee, I'm sorry I can't make the audition but I'm right in the middle of making guacamole!"[7]

A final feature of good interpersonal communication that you can work on right now is the skill of maintaining strong eye contact with the other person. This doesn't mean turning the interview-callback into a stare-you-down game, but simply that you establish direct visual contact with the listener or speaker. This is another aspect that is common to good acting—really look at the other actors as you relate to them onstage. You don't need a handbook like this one to describe how you react to a pair of shifty eyeballs that won't return your gaze, or to a bored and vague stare off into space somewhere when you're trying to talk. Remember that "there's a person inside there" who wants to tell you something important or whom you're trying to reach. So look at the director and talk to that person; reach him with what he wants to know.

All of these features—and so many others that are taught in speech courses—can be contained within the factor common to all human communications situations: one person wants to express something to another. Find out what a person is saying and then respond to it. Find out what you wish to express and then say it. Remember that it is not possible to not communicate. We're always conveying something by language, paralanguage (nonverbal sounds), or body language when speaking and when listening. Learning to control all three levels for effective communication is, of course, a life's work for most of us. But the first step is becoming aware of all the ways we communicate what we know and wish to express.

In the interview-callback situation the fundamental rule of thumb is to be natural and let the director see who you really are. As one coach describes this, "If that is hidden behind a lot of 'pleased-to-meet-yous' and 'thank-you-very-muchs,' you will find . . . that you have lost your chance at a further audition."[8] Nervousness is part of this, of course; often the "thank-you-very-muchs" are simply reassuring clichés we use in order to lessen the tension of a highly artificial situation: "Auditions to me are unreal because nowhere in this world does an actor perform for one or two people. And the person behind the table knows this is unreal, so . . . you need to acknowledge that this is an unreal situation, and won't show me at my best, and that this is understood by the director."[9]

This is a good piece of advice, for casting directors as well as for auditionees. An important corollary is to also acknowledge that whatever is learned from the interview-callback is bound to be only partial understanding, at best. With this always in the back of your mind, be willing to tackle the situation as gamely as possible. After all, you're not approaching a producer as a beggar looking for a handout no matter how much you want to be cast. Producers think they need you or they wouldn't waste time calling you back. This allows the auditionee a certain dignity in the situation, a certain basis for self-confidence.

"Dignity" is a term I encountered frequently while talking to people around the country and working on this handbook.

Actors, of course, are very aware of it because they experience frequent rejections. It's hard to keep your battered ego in shape when people tell you they don't need what you have to offer. To many actors, the name of the game is "who can survive rejections the longest."

Directors speak of an actor's dignity also in the sense of a person's stage presence and the confidence an auditionee can exhibit in a tryout. Acting, after all, is one of the oldest and most challenging, most respected professions in the world. Good directors realize this. The best directors have been actors themselves or else they respect those who are serious about pursuing the profession with commitment and dedication. Acting coaches I've talked with have spoken of the "power" an actor can bring to a scene or a reading onstage, the ability to bring something to life up there which engages our whole interest and excitement. Coaches like Tim Carhart, a Shurtleff "method" teacher at Chicago's Audition Centre, urge the actor to connect his or her sense of pride and confidence to that of the character in the scene; Carhart speaks of "personal power" in a character and in a person that makes him or her act to generate reactions and feelings onstage from the other characters—to create "relationship-producing choices" as character and as a person.[10]

Going into an interview-callback with this sense of "personal power" is important for staying relaxed and for communicating to the director what you can do, and do dependably. If the directors decide after all that you're not what they had in mind or that someone else is better, then you've still got that dignity of being yourself and not someone else's expectations that you've been trying to live up to. "Do what you believe. If you don't get it at least it's for your reasons, and not theirs."[11]

A rejection, after all, is nothing more than a rejection. As Sissy Spacek remarked once on national television: "That can be humiliating. But I think that prepares you for what's to come. A lot of acting is humiliating."[12] Another actor recommends something more positive: "Don't think of it as demeaning yourself. You're not just being nice to someone because you think he can get you somewhere. What you're also doing—and you've got to think of this—is 'I'm giving you the chance to use me.' "[13] Finally, from a major media casting director in New York: "Know what your resources are, what your instrument is. I think if you come out of school with a specific view of what your talent is, you're going to meet with greater success, and you're not going to have to deal with as much of the rejection that most young actors experience."[14]

To conclude, "honest interviewing" is a skill that an actor needs to develop in order to do well in these situations. Being yourself, being natural, and responding honestly to an unreal but necessary encounter with a director is the one area where you should feel most at home. You are (or should be) at home with yourself. Everyone knows the interview-callback is stress producing. Everyone also knows that casting a show in this way—while necessary—is a very risky proposition. And everyone knows too that a one-to-one encounter will reveal strengths and weaknesses on both sides of the casting table. (Why don't those auditionees think of the poor directors on the other side of the desk once in awhile?)

One actor solved the problem of nerves by constantly reminding himself, "The worst thing that could happen is that I wouldn't get the part I already don't have."[15] Eric Morris, a southern California acting coach, reinforces this in very blunt language: "If you expose your limitations and let people see them, you no longer have anything to hide. You're functioning on a level of reality, you can be creative. From a level of phony bullshit you cannot create anything."[16]

The interview-callback, like the actual audition, needs to be carried off with this strong sense of purpose, of belief in the importance—and dignity—of what you're doing. You've boned up and prepared for it, you've gotten some training under your belt. You get down to it and do the best you can with it, and you let the chips fall where they may. Be ready for whatever may happen. And believe in yourself.

Chapter eight

Viewpoints

I've selected the comments in this final chapter to illustrate and emphasize some key points about acting and auditioning. They're not intended to be exhaustive in the sense of saying all one might say about casting plays and how to get roles. That would be impossible. But this handbook has taken a distinct point of view towards auditioning and acting training, and the remarks quoted here all reflect that point of view in one way or another. An undergraduate actor should be disciplined and trained in craft; he or she must also know how to work from the heart instead of relying upon technique alone; and an actor's intelligence must be trained to create focus, shape, and belief in the life of a character—these are a few of the assumptions behind the methods outlined in previous chapters.

Not all the comments to follow are by famous personalities, but all are to the point. And all deserve some meditation/thinking-time from student actors.

Discipline and technique

"One of the worst things that can happen to a beginning, an untrained, actor is to be ratified . . . by blandishments to the effect that there is no such thing as technique; that there is no need to study; that the only way to learn is through doing. . . . This advice creates in the performer a necessary interest in 'knownothingism,' and he or she comes to deny the very existence both of technique and of aesthetics. He or she becomes, in effect, a complete egocentric who is the champion of 'doing what I *feel*,' 'saying what I *feel*,' 'writing what I *feel*.' And the result is more or less harmful garbage."—*David Mamet, playwright*

"Of the thousands of actors and actresses trying to make it, only a small percentage of them do. Why? Is it luck, good timing, discovery in a drugstore, being the producer's son or the director's girl friend? While these things may have helped a few performers initially, what sustained them and made a flash-in-the-pan career into an enduring and viable one is something less romantic and much more grueling and calculated than anyone outside the business realizes. Their secret formula is intelligent, focussed, constant hard work. . . . They figure out *what* they have to work with, *why* and *how* they must work, and *where* and *when* they must work. . . . Gradually it begins to work for them."—*Rebecca Nahas, actor*

"You read a role and in the beginning you're enthused, you're exalted. . . . Then you take the music and you learn it as though you were in the conservatoire. In other words, exactly as it's written, nothing more and nothing less, which is what I call straitjacketing. Having broken this down completely, then you can take wing."—*Maria Callas, actress-singer*

"A few actors have become successful without much training and background, and a lot of people think that this is the fashionable way to do it. But these people who became very successful, people like Gary Cooper, John Wayne, and Clark Gable, had a very special quality. That era is over—the studios don't have the time to nurture talent like they used to. An actor has to be in charge of his life. He has to be tenacious and have a practical, realistic motive. There is a quality about successful people that when things aren't moving for them, they make their own opportunities."—*Burt Metcalfe, producer*

"Actors, great and not-so-great, have been finding their way into the theatre for thousands of years, frequently without the benefit of a teacher's knowledge and guidance. I do not believe any reasonably motivated person can become an actor in the hands of an enlightened teacher. I am convinced that all great actors are born with an unusual gift and aptitude for the profession, and they will find their own way whatever influence a teacher may exert. Many outstanding actors have evolved their own theories and ideas about acting only after years of practicing their craft, while the especially gifted few have been frequently and noticeably inarticulate in trying to explain their art—they simply do it."—*Derek Campbell, actor*

"There's no such thing as film acting or stage acting. There's acting. Some actors say they want to study with someone because they have video. Fine, but first you'd better concentrate on learning how to act, getting the experience of acting, creating a character, learning how to use sense memory. Believe me, being able to act and cold read will get you the job. When you're on the set, most other things are taken care of. It's just a matter of learning how to hit a mark and a bunch of technical things. The key is to be a good actor and not worry about the medium."—*Gary Shaffer, casting director*

"You look very much for swiftness of attack, and the swiftness of feeling, the swiftness of body movement—energy, energy, particularly energy. Where is the energy: vocal? emotional? intellectual? I want somebody who really has energy because acting takes tremendous energy. Most college students don't have any idea of how much energy it takes to do a play. The college student has a lot of physical strength but he doesn't know how to focus it. It's dispersed, or else he thinks it doesn't matter so the script and the moments are under-played, somehow understated. Actors are, like Artaud said, athletes of the heart. You've got to have lots of energy, and auditions really require that." —*Robert Goldsby, Berkeley Stage Co.*

"Think of acting as a business—your business. Never lose your training, your craft, your art: learn to use it in all the various curves that get thrown at you. Your training is yours, no one else's business how you work or prepare. And mind your own business—someone else's ladder and rate of prog-ress has nothing to do with you. But remember: if you lay back, the next guy will overtake you." —*Jane Alderman, casting agent*

Motivation and self-respect

"I think one of the greatest mistakes an actor can make is to do something he doesn't want to do or feels is intrinsically wrong—to allow yourself to be guilted into it. I have done things in dinner theatres that have been less than artistic. But they don't haunt me. And it's not so much that it's a dishonest thing. . . . I feel that if you can make someone forget about their son who died in Viet Nam for a couple of hours or even for fifteen minutes in the second act, then your work had worth. . . . It seems as if any piece you do is an opportunity to communicate something to a group of people." —*Mary Cop-ple, actor*

"Looking back on it, I now say to people who have a kind of juvenile, naive anxiousness about getting there: 'Look—you're in heaven right now. The profession will wait for you, New York City isn't going anywhere, it will wait for you.'

Take your time and study. Students are going to get much
more after they've finished the college experience because
their vision is going to be much more specific, and their awareness, their desire, their feeling of why they must do it. They're
going to be able to articulate their acting career to others and
to themselves so much more clearly. And that's everything—
rather than getting there and being at a disadvantage: unfo-
cussed and sloppy."—*Jack Fletcher, American Conservatory Theatre*

"Your star pupil may have the talent but there's still that huge
element of chance. Another student with less ability may
happen to be the type that is being shopped for in New York
the week after he graduates. They also have to have a large
portion of persistence—the ability to constantly rebuild a faith
in themselves, to overcome what is often perceived to be very
demanding and inhumane. Many decide it's not worth it. My
advice constantly is: 'If it's a happy life you want, and if there's
anything you'd like to do beside this, go do it.' "—*Ned
Schmidtke, Goodman Theatre*

"A good audition never goes unnoticed. It may not achieve
immediate employment, but no director, casting agent, or
composer/lyricist ever forgets first-rate work. There is just too
little of it."—*David Craig, acting coach*

"The number of actors—the number of people who call themselves actors—in this city and in Los Angeles is so huge. It's
the most competitive field in the world, and many people are
unprepared and should not be encouraged because they're
going to be very pained. They're going to have a lot of un-
happiness. I think teachers in the conservatories and in the
liberal arts schools should constantly question what they're
doing, constantly examine why they're putting people out

there for a life of that kind. And unless the student must—
unless a student would die if he didn't—act then he shouldn't
act. I face actors, desperate actors, constantly, and I think that
educators have a responsibility to these people."—*Rosemary
Tischler, casting director*

"My work is a means to an end, not an end. The end is my
life. Acting is a very good tool for acquiring independence.
It forces you to be constantly examining how you react in
different situations. Besides talent, an actor or actress has to
have an incredible amount of stamina and the ability to adapt.
I consider those to be life lessons. It's very tough to last in
this business. It's easy to be successful quickly but very hard
to remain human."—*Susan Sarandon, actress*

"There's a certain chemistry to an actor when he walks onstage. He alters the state of the stage; he has the potential to
make everything shift."—*Michael Leibert, Berkeley Repertory
Theatre*

"I would be truly ashamed if an actor told me a part of mine
wasn't, in the real sense, big enough—even though, often as
not, the actor will prove to be foolish enough to have counted
the lines and not the heartbeats of the part."—*Peter Shaffer,
playwright*

"Most people who call themselves actors are either untrained
or unprepared emotionally for the job. We have created a
position in the common man's life that cannot be filled by
anyone else but actors, and that is escape into someone else's
dilemma and away from your own. . . . The danger is that
people are allowing actors to do all the feeling, all the acting
out of life, while they sit passively by."—*Barry Bostwick, actor*

"It's worth it if you make it. It might even be worth it if you don't because if you don't there are other things to do that are close enough within the business that are satisfying."— *Bert Convy, actor*

"The hard ones are when you keep reading and get down to the last callback and somebody else gets it. But the thing you have to remember is that if you do get two or more callbacks you *do* have the ability. If you don't get the role after that it's only because for some reason you don't have the look or the voice. But it has nothing to do with your ability. *Nothing.* And you have to keep telling yourself that. Before I go out on a reading I tell myself I have to give one hundred percent; if I don't, there are two million other people out there who will!"—*Valerie Landsburg, actor*

Confidence in using your self

"Most actors have learned to 'perform' at auditions in order to reassure producers, directors, and authors who are normally more terrified than the actor himself, if the actor could only so realize. But such 'performances' are parodies, and the director who does not invite them will be given a great deal more."—*William Redfield, actor*

"Speech is speaking a language locked beneath it. That is its continual reference. The speech we hear is an indication of what we don't hear. It is a necessary avoidance, a violent, sly, anguished, or mocking smoke-screen which keeps the other in its place. One way of looking at speech is to say it is a constant stratagem to cover nakedness."—*Harold Pinter, playwright*

"The novice . . . retreats from his own insecurity, and lack of proper training and control. He may know what he wants to say; he is often very articulate and has an excellent command of language, but he feels that he must be someone else, that he himself is not good enough when facing an audience. You cannot become an accomplished speaker overnight, but when you have developed and integrated all your skills and abolished stereotyped habit patterns, the whole person that you communicate most effectively will be yourself—yourself at peak but still yourself."—*Arthur Lessac, coach*

"What television is feeding us . . . is a kind of TV dinner, and it tells everyone who is watching it that there is nothing beyond the TV dinner—just stick it in the oven, get it fast, and eat it. There is nothing about developing a sensuality or spirituality, nothing to tell them that what makes them unique is their individual passion for life, their ability to remain vulnerable no matter what hits. I know that's hard, it's very hard. We all have masks and we have to. But it's very difficult to be with people who are constantly what they wish to present, because finally they are simply their presentation."—*Colleen Dewhurst, actress*

"You are what you are, and you go out on the stage using what you have been using all your life because *that* is the thing which I think is much more pertinent than something temporary like a quick moustache, a quick funny look, or a funny walk. . . . Once I realized that I had inside myself everything that was required for almost every part ever written. . . .Once you realize that the potential to be that is inside yourself, then acting becomes easier. It becomes releasing, and you become your own psychiatrist in a way."—*Ian McKellen, actor*

"In order to become a great actress you have to work very hard. You have to learn to discover the feelings inside of people which they try very hard to hide. You have to find and love the goodness which is inside even the cruelest person, and you have to find and understand the badness which is inside (even just a little bit) even the best people . . . and most important, you must learn to see inside yourself and to understand your own feelings. . . . Great actors are not great because they sing well or dance well; they are great because their ability to see inside the thoughts of people is great. I truly believe if you work on that ability to see inside and to understand people, that success will come to you, perhaps in a surprising way and at a surprising time."—*David Han-hilammi, director*

"When I write for *M*A*S*H* I'm very interested in finding the flaws in the Hawkeye character. I really don't believe that people are heroes. The best of people do things that are regrettable. And I think that's what drama is all about—seeing decent people do regrettable things. . . . Just as the characters I write have good qualities and flaws, I see the same mixture in myself. In fact, I drew on some of my own flaws in writing those characters."—*Alan Alda, actor-producer-director*

"If we ever say the word 'character' we put it in quotes because why destroy the ultimate bonding by insisting that it is somebody else? I mean, you're the only person up there—you're their Hamlet. Whatever you do is what Hamlet is doing."—*Tim Carhart, actor-auditions coach*

"The point is that we all have inner voices—some not so nice as others. And if we are lucky enough to grow up and reach any level of maturity we come to terms with those voices and we become a whole person, a person made up of these voices. I find that quite satisfying."—*David Rounds, actor*

"The purpose of performing is to derive pleasure for yourself as well as give the best you can to the public, the best of what the piece is about. It's a hell of a lot of energy one musters out of emotions, physically, intellectually, emotionally. The point is to do well for yourself. I mean, if you don't derive any pleasure from it, forget it!"—*Maria Ewing, actress-singer*

"It is difficult to distinguish between moving decisively and moving out of fear. If you know what to do, don't vacillate."
—*Hal Prince, director-producer*

"You have to be willing to make a fool of yourself. The world of commercials, film and theatre is very similar. It gives us a chance to play 'let's pretend' for the rest of our lives. It allows us to be children forever—to live out someone's fantasies—but at the same time it gives us the opportunity to use the talent we have in portraying many different characters. It also means that if you really want that job, you've got to be willing to make a fool of yourself. The financial reward can make it all worthwhile."—*Iris Acker, actress-coach*

"Truth is not limited to an actor fulfilling himself with the joy that he has felt something for the first time, for crying out loud. I mean, you have 'felt' since the time you were born. This marvelous technique of Stanislavski just puts you in an easy connection with those experiences which you already have. If you cannot get to them in a direct kind of way and have them at hand, you shouldn't be in the acting profession to begin with. . . . How do I *project* that? That is the beginning. How do I communicate that to those people out there? Theatre is communication."—*Jose Quintero, director*

"I don't choose people, the people choose themselves. When they stand up there and you see their eyes, their demeanor and the way they hold their head, you pretty well know it when a person belongs. It's something *they* do. The way in which they stand and look and talk to you. Even the way in which they hand their music to the accompanist is all part of the audition process. Although we finally select them, they do a great deal to help us make that choice."—*Jay Blackton, casting director*

"Remember that on a resume or in an interview you're dealing with people whose *life work* is recognizing a subtext between the lines. So be honest in presenting yourself. No 'stock answers' are permitted here."—*Jane Armitage, casting director*

"There are no golden rules when it comes to auditioning. Why? Largely because a good audition doesn't always guarantee a good performance. In fact, some of the very best auditions, and those that led to my casting the person, often in turn led to bland performances. Certainly when it comes to the classics, an actor should have facility and experience with verse. But even then I've cast individuals with little or no experience with the Bard and gotten superlative work from them because they had guts, intelligence, a dash of talent, and what I call passionate intensity: the four ingredients that in the end can melt down the doors of any casting office and blow away the golden rules at any open call."—*W. Stuart McDowell, artistic director*

Appendix A

Scenes and Monologues

Same Time, Next Year by Bernard Slade

George and Doris; male and female in their thirties; comic. George tries to tell his lover an unkind story about his wife.

Doris: Harry's home a lot. The insurance business has been kind of slow lately.

George: How does he feel about all this?

Doris: When I told him I wanted to go back to school because I wanted some identity, he lost his temper and said, "You want identity? Go build a bridge! Invent penicillin, but get off my back!"

George: I always said Harry had a good head on his shoulders.

Doris: George, that was the *bad* story about him. How's Helen?

George: Helen's fine. Just fine.

Doris: Tell me a story that shows how really lousy she can be.

George: (*Surprised.*) That's not like you.

Doris: We seem to need something to bring us closer together.

George: I don't understand.

Doris: I thought a really bad story about Helen might

173

George: make you appreciate me more. *(This finally gets a small smile from George.)*

George: Okay. *(Doris sits with her drink and listens.)* As you know, she has this funny sense of humor.

Doris: By funny I take it you mean peculiar?

George: Right. And it comes out at the most inappropriate times. I had signed this client—very proper, very old money. Helen and I were invited out to his house for cocktails to get acquainted with him and his wife. Well, it was all pretty awkward but we managed to get through the drinks all right. Then as we went to leave, instead of walking out the front door, I walked into the hall closet. Now that wasn't so bad—I mean anybody can do that. The mistake I made was that I *stayed* in there.

Doris: You stayed in the closet?

George: Yes. I don't know—I guess I figured they hadn't noticed, and I'd stay there until they'd gone away—okay, I admit I didn't think things through. I was in there for about a minute before I realized I'd misjudged the situation. When I came out the three of them were staring at me. All right, it was an embarrassing situation but I probably could have carried it off. Except for Helen. You know what she did?

Doris: What?

George: She peed on the carpet.

Doris: *(Incredulous.)* She did what?

George: Oh, not right away. First of all, she started to laugh. Her face was all screwed up and the laughter was sort of—squeaky. Then she held her stomach and tears started to roll down her face. Then she peed on their Persian rug. *(Doris is having trouble keeping a straight face.)*

Doris: What did you say?

George: I said, "You'll have to excuse my wife. Ever since her last pregnancy she's had a problem" Then I offered to have the rug cleaned.

Doris: Did that help?

George: They said it wasn't necessary. They had a maid.

(Doris finally explodes into peals of laughter.) You
think that's funny.

Doris: I've been meaning to tell you this for years, but I
think I'd like Helen.

George: *(Irritated.)* Would she come off any worse if I told
you I lost the account.

Doris: George, when did you get so *stuffy?*

George: Stuffy? Just because I don't like my wife urinating
on my clients' carpets does not mean I'm stuffy!

Doris: Okay, maybe not just that but—well—look at
you. *(She gets up, gestures at him.)* I mean—Jesus—
you scream Establishment.

Denotative paraphrase: George, from *Same Time, Next Year*

Helen has a strange sense of humor and . . . creates very
embarrassing situations. One time I'd just closed a deal
with a very important and well-established client. We went
to the client's home for dinner and I was very nervous, and
I absentmindedly opened the door to the hall closet instead
of the front door on our way out. That's an honest mistake,
but I stayed in there for about one minute . . . I was confused, you see, and when I came out it was somewhat embarrassing. Everyone stared at me, but the worst thing was
that Helen . . . she urinated on their carpet . . . she started
laughing at me and convulsing so hard, and then shedding
tears in hysterics. And then she actually urinated over the
client's Persian rug.

Connotative paraphrase: George, from *Same Time, Next Year*

Helen has a sense of humor like you wouldn't believe, I
mean she's just bizarre at times. One time, for instance, I
had this deal going and we were out to dinner with this

super important client of mine. And what happened was that on the way out of the guy's house I accidentally walked through the closet door instead of the front door. Well, that was a shocker of course. I mean, like it took me a minute to figure out what had happened . . . and when I walked out they were all looking at me like I was drunk or crazy or something. Well, I suppose that would have been OK, except for what Helen did then . . . it was bad enough, I mean, without Helen pissing all over the guy's rug she was laughing so hard at me . . . I mean she started screwing her face up in giggles and then holding her sides all over, and her tears streaming down, like she was cracking up! And she just couldn't stand it any more, she was laughing so hard at me that she just let go and pissed all over this dude's expensive Persian rug. I mean, she is weird sometimes!

Gemini by Albert Innaurato

Judith and Francis; female and male in their twenties; seriocomic.

Judith:	Do I bore you? Do you think I'm ugly? Do I have bad breath?
Francis:	Oh, come on!
Judith:	Hey, Francis, we're just alike, can't you see that?
Francis:	Oh yeah.
Judith:	Two overachievers. Really. I know my family is better off than yours; but we're just alike, and there was something last winter and now you're telling me . . .
Francis:	Look, I'm going to be twenty-one tomorrow. Well . . . I don't know what to say.
Judith:	Is there a reason?
Francis:	I don't think I can say.
Judith:	That doesn't make any sense.
Francis:	I think I'm queer.
Judith:	Why don't we back up a bit. I said: "We're just alike et cetera" and you said you were going to be twenty-one tomorrow, and I looked at you

	with deep-set sea-blue eyes, and you said . . .
Francis:	I think I'm queer.
Judith:	*(Laughs.)* Well, I guess we can't get around it. Do you want to amplify? I mean this seems like quite a leap from what I remember of those long, sweet, ecstatic nights, naked in each other's young arms, clinging to . . .
Francis:	We fucked. Big deal. That's what kids are supposed to do. And be serious.
Judith:	I am serious. Is there a particular boy?
Francis:	Yes.
Judith:	An adolescent, a German Adolescent . . .
Francis:	Not German, no.
Judith:	Do I know him? *(Francis doesn't answer.)* Reciprocal?
Francis:	It was just this spring. He began to haunt me. We became friends. We talked a lot—late in my room when you were studying. Well, I don't know, and you see—I've had, well, crushes before. I dreamed of him. It's not reciprocal, no, he doesn't know, but it became more and more obvious to me. I mean, I'd look at him, and then some other boy would catch my eye and I'd think—you see?
Judith:	Well, I suppose I could start teaching you the secrets of makeup. *(Francis turns away, annoyed.)* Well, how do you expect me to react? You seem to think I ought to leap out the window because of it. But it's like you're suddenly turning to me and saying you are from Mars. Well, you might be, but I don't see much evidence and I can't see what difference it makes. I'm talking about you and me, I and thou and all that. Alright, maybe you do have an eye for the boys, well so do I, but you . . . you are special to me. I wouldn't throw you over just because a hockey player looked good. Why do you have to give me up?
Francis:	I don't think that makes any sense, Judith. I mean, if I were from Mars, it would make a difference. I'd have seven legs and talk a different

	language and that's how I feel now. *(Judith embraces him.)* Don't touch me so much, Judith, and don't look at me . . .
Judith:	Then you're afraid. That explains that fat and ugly nonsense and this sudden homosexual panic. You're afraid that anyone who responds to you will make demands you can't meet. You're afraid you'll fail . . .
Francis:	Good evening, Ladies and Gentlemen, Texaco presents: "Banality on Parade!"
Judith:	You're afraid to venture. That's why you've enshrined someone who doesn't respond to you, probably doesn't even know you're interested. If the relationship never happens, you are never put to the test and can't fail. The Overachiever's Great Nightmare!
Francis:	That's crazy!
Judith:	I bet this boy who draws you is some Harvard sprite, a dew-touched freshman . . .
Francis:	He was a freshman.
Judith:	In Randy's class and that proves it. Look at Randy—what kind of response could someone like that have but the giggles? And you know that. You're afraid of commitment.

The Duchess of Malfi by John Webster

The Duchess; a woman in her late twenties or thirties; serious.
The duchess confesses her love and proposes to Antonio.

The misery of us that are born great!
We are forced to woo, because none dare woo us;
And as a tyrant doubles with his words
And fearfully equivocates, so we
Are forced to express our violent passions
In riddles and in dreams, and leave the path
Of simple virtue, which was never made
To seem the thing it is not. Go, go brag
You have left me heartless; mine is in your bosom:

I hope 'twill multiply love there. You do tremble.
Make not your heart so dead a piece of flesh,
To fear more than to love me. Sir, be confident,
What is it distracts you? This is flesh and blood, sir;
'Tis not the figure cut in alabaster
Kneels at my husband's tomb. Awake, awake, man!
I do here put off all vain ceremony
And only do appear to you a young widow
That claims you for her husband; and, like a widow,
I use but half a blush in it.

Denotative paraphrase: *The Duchess of Malfi*

It's really hard to be rich and to have an important family. I
have to be somewhat aggressive because men think I'm
sort of aloof and untouchable and that I probably have
everything I need; and like some kind of hypocrite with
two-faced words I have to hide my love, and my feelings,
behind jokes and stories, and be dishonest—as though
anyone can be honest. You're probably going to run out
and tell everyone what a pushover I am. Well, you have
pushed me over. I do love you, and I hope you love me
too. You're trembling. Don't be uptight! It's all right.
What's wrong? I'm just a woman, a real person and not
some news photo of someone kneeling at my husband's
grave. Hey come on, you know what I'm saying. I'm a
young widow who'd love to be your wife, and just like a
widow, I'm only half ashamed to say so.

Connotative paraphrase: *The Duchess of Malfi*

God! This is such a drag! What is happening to me? What
am I doing? I must be crazy—why the hell *should* I feel
guilty being sexually aggressive if I want to? If I need to? I

mean, what's wrong with it? At least it's honest even though this sexist society doesn't even want to think about it! Haven't I got a right to express my needs like everyone else? Even if I am a "duchess" I'm still a person, for Christ sake! And so I have to use polite words to hustle you, Antonio. I do what I feel I have to, the only way I can do it. And hell—you don't understand, do you? Freaks you out, does it? You don't really understand me as a person either, do you? Oh God, I want you so much, Antonio. Can't you turn on to that? Get it on! I'm talking like a woman, a female, not like a duchess. Let's just cut through all the crap and get down to a relationship! Something more special, more real and honest between us. I mean, what is "nobility" anyway? It's leadership, isn't it? Courage, vision, presence of mind more than the average—aren't those part of it? And that's why I'm coming at you now. Have you got the guts to do it with me, or would you feel safer keeping it all just "comfortable" between us?

No Place to Be Somebody by Charles Gordone

Johnny; a black male in his twenties; serious. Johnny threatens to kill his old friend for betraying him.

See this, Sweets? My firs' an' only pistol. You gave it to me long time ago when I was a lookout for you when you was pullin' them owl jobs in Queens. I worshipped the groun' you walked on. I thought the sun rose an' set in yo' ass. You showed me how to make thirteen straight passes without givin' up the dice. Stood behin' me an' nudged me when to play my ace. Hipped me how to make a gapers cut. How to handle myself in a pill joint. Taught me to trust no woman over six or under sixty. Turned me on to the best horse players an' number runners. Showed me how to keep my ass-pocket full'a coins without going to

jail. Said the wors' crime I ever committed was comin'
out'a my mama screamin' black. Tole me all about white
folks an' what to expect from the best of 'em. You said as
long as there was a single white man on this earth, the
black man only had one free choice. That was the way he
died. When you went to jail for shootin' Cholly you said,
"Sonny Boy, git us a plan." Well, I got us a plan.

The Basic Training of Pavlo Hummel by David Rabe

*Pavlo; a man in his twenties; serious. Pavlo tries to tell his
brother that the army has changed him.*

Look at me! I'm different! I'm different than I was! *(This is
with fury.)* I'm not the same anymore. I was an asshole. I'm
not an asshole anymore. I'm not an asshole anymore! *(Silence as he stares in anguish.)* I came here to forgive you. I
don't need you anymore. *(Rapidly, in a rush of words.)* I'm
happier now than I ever was, I got people who respect me.
Lots of 'em. There was this guy . . . he was gonna kill me,
he said. Everybody tried to stop me because this guy had
hurt a lot of people already and he had this uncle who's
taught him all about fightin' and this uncle had been exe-
cuted in San Quentin for killing people. We went out back
of the barracks. It went on and on, hitting and kicking. It
went on and on; all around the barracks. The crowd right
with us. And then . . . all of a sudden . . . this look came
into his eye . . . and he just stopped . . . and reached
down to me and hugged me. He just hugged and hugged
me. And that look was in all their eyes. All the soldiers. I
don't need you anymore, Mickey. I got real brothers now.
No big thing. We got the same mother; that's shit enough.
I'm gonna shower and shave, okay? Then we can go out
drinkin'.

A Midsummer Night's Dream by Shakespeare

Puck; young male or female; comic. Oberon's fairy assistant finds the lovers asleep in the wood and sprinkles the love potion upon their eyes.

> Through the forest have I gone,
> But Athenian found I none,
> On whose eyes I might approve
> This flower's force in stirring love,
> Night and silence.—Who is here?
> Weeds of Athens he doth wear:
> This is he, my master said,
> Despised the Athenian maid;
> And here the maiden, sleeping sound,
> On the dank and dirty ground.
> Pretty soul! She durst not lie
> Near this lack-love, this kill-courtesy.
> Churl, upon thy eyes I throw
> All the power this charm doth owe.
> When thou wak'st, let love forbid.
> Sleep his seat on thy eyelid.
> So awake when I am gone,
> For I must now to Oberon.

Two Gentlemen of Verona by Shakespeare

Launcelot Gobbo; a young man; comic. Launcelot delivers a comic monologue to the audience during which he explains how he saved his dog, Crab, from a whipping.

When a man's servant shall play the cur with him, look you, it goes hard: one that I brought up of a puppy; one that I saved from drowning, when three or four of his blind brothers and sisters went to it! I have taught him, even as one would say precisely, "thus I would teach a dog." I was sent to deliver him as a present to Mistress Silvia from my master; and I came no sooner into the dining chamber, but he steps me to her trencher, and steals her capon's leg. He thrusts himself into the company of three or four gentlemanlike dogs, under the duke's table: he had not been there—bless the mark—a pissing while, but all the chamber smelt him. "Out with the dog!" says one: "What cur is that?" says another: "Whip him out," says the third: "Hang him up," says the duke. I, having been acquainted with the smell before, knew it was Crab, and goes me to the fellow that whips the dogs: "Friend," quoth I, "you mean to whip the dog?" "Ay, marry, do I," quoth he. "You do him the more wrong," quoth I; " 'twas I did the thing you wot of." He makes me no more ado, but whips me out of the chamber. How many masters would do this for his servant?

Exercise for "beats"

When a man's servant shall play the cur with him, look you, it goes hard: one that I brought up of a puppy; one that I saved from drowning, when three or four of his blind brothers and sisters went to it! I have taught him, even as one would say precisely, "thus I would teach a dog,"	*to brag*
I was sent to deliver him as a present to Mistress Silvia from my master; and I came no sooner into the dining chamber, but he steps me to her trencher, and steals her capon's leg. He thrusts himself into the company of three or four gentlemanlike dogs, under the duke's table: he had not been there—bless the mark—a pissing while, but all the chamber smelt him. "Out with the dog!" says one: "What cur is that?" says another: "Whip him out," says the third: "Hang him up," says the duke.	*to shock his listeners*
I, having been acquainted with the smell before, knew it was Crab, and goes me to the fellow that whips the dogs: "Friend," quoth I, "you mean to whip the dog?" "Ay, marry, do I," quoth he. "You do him the more wrong," quoth I; "'twas I did the thing you wot of." He makes no more ado, but whips me out of the chamber.	*to play the hero*
How many masters would do this for his servant?	*to ask for support*

Uncommon Women by Wendy Wasserstein

Muffet; a woman in her twenties; seriocomic.

I am so tired. Why doesn't someone just take me away
from all this? Did you ever notice how walking into Samantha's room is like walking into a clean sheet? She and Susie
Friend celebrate Piglet's birthday. Katie says you're very
bright. Did I tell you what happened in Chip Knowles'
women's history class today? Do you know Chip Knowles?
He always wears chamois shirts and Topsiders from L.L.
Bean. You can never find anything you want in those L.L.
Bean catalogues. So I just order a decoy duck every year. It
makes me feel waspy. Chip's wife, Libby, graduated first in
her class from Vassar. When I told Chip I was a senior and
didn't know what I'd be doing next year, Chip told me that
Libby doesn't really spend the day mopping and catching
tadpoles with Chip, Jr. She may be mopping with her
hands but with her mind she's reliving the water imagery
in the *Faerie Queen.* Anyway, I thought women's history
would be a gut and it wouldn't look as obvious on my record as "Marriage and the Family." As it turns out, this
class isn't half bad. We read all the basics; the womb-penis
inner and outer space nonsense. *The Feminine Mystique, Sexual Politics,* Mabel Dodge's *Diary.* Chip Knowles says wom-
en's history is relevant. Do you think women will lose their
relevancy in five years? Like "Car 54, Where Are You?"
Anyway, after two months of reading about suffragettes
and courageous choices, this French dish comes into class
dressed in a tight turtleneck and skirt. And you know how
for seminar breaks everyone brings in graham crackers,
well this chick brings in homemade petit-fours. And she
stands in front of the class and tells us she has not prepared her report on Rosie the Riveter because, "You girls
are wasting your time. You should do more avec what you
have down here *(Muffet points to her breasts)* than avec what
you have up here." *(Muffet points to her head.)* And in less

than five seconds the class is giving her a standing ovation, everyone is applauding. Except Holly and Rita, who grabbed the petit-fours, and ran out of the room in protest. I didn't do anything. I felt so confused. I mean this chick is an obvious imbecile. But I didn't think she was entirely wrong either. I guess the truth is men are very important to me. Well, not more important than you and Holly and Samantha. Well, not always, pumpkin. Sometimes I know who I am when I feel attractive. Other times it makes me feel very shallow like I'm not Rosie the Riveter. I suppose this isn't a very impressive sentiment, but I would really like to meet my prince. Even a few princes. And I wouldn't give up being a person. I'd still remember all the Art History dates. I just don't know why suddenly I'm supposed to know what I want to do. I guess I should think about sleeping with someone tonight to pass the time. Except it's always creepy in the morning. Rita doesn't think so. But she's promiscuous. I'm not promiscuous. I just hate going to bed alone.

Love Rides the Rails by Hugh Nevill

Prudence and Truman; female and male in their twenties; comic.

Prudence: (*Entering left, panting.*) Truman! Truman Pendennis! Where are you?
Truman: (*Muffled by gag.*) Here!
Prudence: (*Going to him.*) Mr. Pendennis, are you hurt?
Truman: (*Still muffled.*) No, but . . . (*Train whistle sounds quite close.*)
Prudence: Oh, sir, I will remove the gag. (*Does so.*)
Truman: Prudence! Miss Prudence! How come you here?
Prudence: I saw you from yonder hilltop. Have the villains wounded you, sir?
Truman: No, but I am fast bound to these iron rails. And

hark! The train approaches! *(Train sounds closer still, left.)*

Prudence: Let me free you, sir. *(Speaking as she works.)* Who were the base cowards who attacked you, sir?

Truman: Simon Darkway and his creature, Dirk Sneath.

Prudence: Those two? Oh, horror!

Truman: First they caused a strike, then by foul means plunged me into disgrace. Now, when that failed, they planned to wreck the mail-train and rob us of our franchise.

Prudence: Oh, sir, I have indeed been blind.

Truman: You knew not the wickedness of this world.

Prudence: *(Standing up.)* Heaven has opened my eyes and I know you for the true man you are.

Truman: *(Standing up.)* Miss Prudence!

Prudence: Mr. Pendennis! *(They are about to embrace when train whistle is heard closer still.)*

Truman: The train! We must stop the train! See, the rail is cut!

Prudence: Oh, sir, what can we do?

Truman: I will repair the track. Do you take down yonder green lamp and set in its place the red. *(Starts work on track.)*

Prudence: *(After picking up green lamp.)* But where is the red lamp, sir?

Truman: I had it with me—but wait! Those villains carried it away!

Prudence: But, sir, we must stop the train!

Truman: But how? Unless they see the red light, they will think the track is clear and hurtle onward to death and destruction.

Prudence: Could you not shout, sir? Wave your arms in warning?

Truman: They would not see until too late. The night is dark.

Prudence: Oh, sir, we are undone!

Truman: Had I but a scarf—a kerchief of red! I could wrap it round the lantern and it would suffice.

Prudence: A scarf! A kerchief! *(She looks down.)* Oh, Mr. Pendennis! *(Train whistle closer still. Use approach-*

ing train effect and start it here—building to en-
trance of engine.)
Truman: Yes, Miss Prudence?
Prudence: You asked for something red—there is . . . my
skirt!
Truman: Your skirt! No, that cannot be!
Prudence: But sir, it must be if we are to save the railroad.
Truman: But there will be *men* on that train—*men* who
will see your . . .
Prudence: He *(Pointing heavenward.)* will forgive and under-
stand. And my dear dead father. *(Making moth-*
er's gesture.) God rest his saintly soul—
Truman: *(Hurriedly.)* Amen!
Prudence: —would have wished it.
Truman: But your gentle upbringing, your modesty?
Prudence: Shall prudish modesty send those men to their
death? *(Loud whistle off left.)* No, no, a thousand
times no! *(Starts to remove skirt. Piano chord.)*
Truman: Miss Prudence! *(Turns away and hides eyes.)*

Tom Paine by Paul Foster

Count; male or female; comic. Louis XVI; male or female; comic.

Count: Sire, last night I had a dream. A divine inspiration worthy of your attention.
Louis XVI: Invent for me a knife big enough to cut loose
that miserable little English island tied to the
coast of our France and let it float to . . . to
Terre de Fuego.
Count: Sire, I cannot do that. Besides, your brother-in-
law owns Terre de Fuego.
Louis XVI: Bien, then it would be his problem.
Count: We can do better than that. We can keep this
little war in America boiling by giving the rebels monies to purchase ammunition, gunpow-

der, boots and thereby divert enough of the English armies to fight the rebels, so they will not be a threat to your Majesty. We give this to the rebels under the fictitious name of Hortalez and Company, so the British spies will never know the money comes from us. And who knows, the rebels might even win. And who knows, he *(Pointing to George III.)* might even lose his American Colonies. What do you think that would do to his gout?

Louis XVI: How much will your "divine inspiration" cost us?

Count: About two million livres.

Louis XVI; Deux million! You and your divine inspiration are crazy!

Count: But you see, Sire, we would give the rebels all the army's outdated ammunition which we would have to melt anyway. They will do the fighting for us. And you can appreciate what the loss of America would mean to the King.

Louis XVI: Divine inspiration!

Count: I am pleased you like my plan.

Louis XVI: Whose plan?

Count: Your plan, Sire. We will use Beaumarchais.

Louis XVI: That clockmaker. I can't stand him.

Count: Exactly, Sire. If anything goes wrong, he will be the ah . . . ah . . .

Both: . . . the ah . . . *(Laugh.)* the scapegoat.

Louis XVI: I love it. Call him in.

The Woods by David Mamet

Ruth and Nick; female and male; serious.

Ruth: Are you mad at me?

Nick: No.

Ruth: Do you want to go in?

Nick: No. *(Pause.)*

Ruth: What do you want? *(Pause.)* Come on, we'll go inside.

Nick: Why?

Ruth: I don't know. We'll make a sandwich.

Nick: Why?

Ruth: Because if you were hungry.

Nick: Well, I'm not.

Ruth: Okay. Okay. We have to talk. I have to talk to you. *(Pause.)* Gimme some.

Nick: You're drunk.

Ruth: I am not, Gimme some. *(He gives her some wine.)* All right. Siddown. Look: are you cold?

Nick: Yes.

Ruth: All right, then. Look. You stay here, I am going to get you something. Stay here. *(She goes inside, and comes out and hands him a package.)* This is for you. *(Pause.)*

Nick: What is it?

Ruth: Just open it. *(Pause.)* Open it and then we'll talk. *(He opens it. He takes out a bracelet. He examines it.)*

Nick: It's very nice. *(Pause. He continues to examine the bracelet.)* Is it gold? *(Pause.)*

Ruth: Read it.

Nick: "Nicholas. *(Pause.)* I will always love you. Ruth." *(A long pause.)*

Ruth: Put it on.

Nick: *(Very softly.)* No.

Ruth: Then go fuck yourself. Look: you don't understand. You don't know me. You don't. You think that I'm stupid. You do. You think that. Don't you?

Nick: No.

Ruth: Yeah, you do. You don't know, you don't know a thing. Look. Look. Look, Nick. I love you. I love you so much. I just want to be with you. That's the only thing I want to do. I do not want to hurt you. *(Pause.)* Do you want to make love to me?

Nick: No. *(Pause.)*

Ruth: You don't want to make love to me?

Nick: No.

Ruth: You know that I want you, Nick. You know that. *(Pause.)* Why do you think I came up with you?

Nick: Why?

Ruth: Do you care?

Nick: Why did you come up?

Ruth: You don't know why I did? Are you dumb? What do you mean? *(Pause.)* Caw caw caw the gulls fly. They eat fish?

Nick: I don't know.

Ruth: They either eat the fish or insects. *(Pause.)* We eat fish. The fish eat seaweed. It all dies, the things turn into shells. *(Pause.)* Or deposits. They wash up. As coral. Maybe they make sand, or special beaches. They decay and wash away. *(Pause.)* Then they form the islands. *(Pause.)* Nothing lasts forever. *(Pause.)* Don't make me go home. *(Pause.)* I want to live with you. Go put it on.

Nick: I know some things that you don't know.

Ruth: Things. *(Pause.)* You don't know anything. *(Pause.)* You don't even know what's good for you, you come up here with all those other, I don't know and the only woman who loves you and you don't know shit. You think I'm stupid. *(Pause.)* You never had this. You're the one that's stupid.

Nick: Do you know that you demean yourself?

Ruth: I do?

Nick: Yes.

Ruth: Isn't that too bad.

Nick: It is.

Ruth: You don't have any feelings.

Nick: I have feelings.

Ruth: What are they? *(Pause.)* What are they? You think that you have feelings. Why do we come up here if you're so upset the whole time, that's what I would like to know.

Nick: Why? *(Pause.)*

Ruth: You asked me. I am your guest up here. You're bored or what, what am I s'posed to do, go off and drown myself somewhere? I am your guest. We could be many things to one another. *(Pause.)* In our friendship. You have no idea of the possibilities. *(Pause.)* Do you know that?

Nick: Why don't you leave me alone? *(Pause.)*

Ruth: I will. *(Pause.)* I don't like to be in places where I don't feel good. When's the next bus?

Nick: In the morning.

Ruth: Well, I'm going to take it. So that's it. So you can just relax. I've had enough of this. *(Pause.)* Life goes on. Drip drip. Drip drip. Do you feel better now?

Nick: Yes.

Ruth: Good. *(Pause.)* I care how you feel. We have to learn from things. *(Pause.)* Do you think that?

Nick: Yes. I do.

Ruth: Yes. I do, too. *(Pause.)* Many things go on. We have to learn from them. Good. Good.

Nick: *(Pause. They sit for a moment then she gets up to go in.)* Where are you going?

Ruth: In. I have to pack.

Objectives and concrete actions in *The Woods*

Nick

- he has other important problems on his mind (he paces restlessly and changes stage positions frequently, he pretends to be preoccupied with a book or a magazine for part of the scene, he speaks in a clipped and impatient fashion in order to cut short the subjects of her conversation);
- he wants to get rid of her but doesn't know how to tell her (he moves around the stage to avoid her when she draws close, he frequently stares at her as if she were some strange apparition on the porch of his cottage, he speaks condescendingly to her by patiently spelling things out clearly and succinctly);
- he's struggling to find meaning and stimulation in this too-familiar situation (he may begin the scene by

trying to get physical with her and then gradually
lose interest, he may frequently struggle for the right
words to say but never quite find them, he may listen closely to her but just draw a frustrating blank
when he must respond to what she says).

Ruth

- she is playfully trying to get a rise out of him (she
  may work at him physically from all sides, she may
  frequently "play-act" as she invents one thing after
  another to interest him, she may often use the wine
  glass when she registers his total lack of response);
- she is trying to hit upon something meaningful in
  their present boring situation (she may physically approach and withdraw sexually in one or two sections,
  she may gush words neurotically as she seeks to verbalize something important that may still exist between them, she may frequently punctuate her
  words with explosive and violent gestures);
- she wants to win back his love (she eagerly intro-
  duces one "caring" subject after another to show her
  affection, she may try to quietly stand physically
  close to him except for a few moments of impatient
  outbursts, she may occasionally adjust her clothing
  or pay some critical attention to her physical appearance during the scene in order to seem more attractive).

Camelot by Lerner and Loewe

Arthur and Guenevere; male and female; comic.

Arthur: A thousand pardons, Milady. Wait! Don't run.
           *(She stops in the corner of the stage and looks at
           him, cowering.)* Please! I won't harm you.

Guenevere:	You lie! You'll leap at me and throw me to the ground.
Arthur:	*(Amazed, protesting.)* I won't do any such thing. *(He takes a step toward her. She takes a step backwards. He stops.)*
Guenevere:	Then you'll twist my arm and tie me to a tree.
Arthur:	But I won't.
Guenevere:	Then you'll sling me over your shoulder and carry me off.
Arthur:	No, no, no! I swear it! By the Sword Excalibur! I swear I won't touch you.
Guenevere:	*(Hurt.)* Why not? *(Sudden rage.)* How dare you insult me in this fashion. Do my looks repel you?
Arthur.	No. You're beautiful.
Guenevere:	Well, then? We're alone. I'm completely defenseless. What kind of a cad are you? Apologize at once.
Arthur:	*(At once.)* I apologize. I'm not certain what I've done, but from the depths of my heart, I apologize.
Guenevere:	*(With sudden wisdom.)* Ah! I think I know. You heard my praying.
Arthur:	I couldn't help it, Milady. You prayed rather loudly.
Guenevere:	And you know who I am.
Arthur:	You're Guenevere.
Guenevere:	Yes, of course. You're afraid because I may be your queen. That accounts for your respectful, polite, despicable behaviour.
Arthur:	Milady, I would never harm you for any reason. And as for what to do with you, I'm at a loss. I know you are to be queen, and I should escort you back to your carriage. At the same time, you're a maiden in genuine distress. It's chivalry versus country. I can't quite determine which call to obey.
Guenevere:	*(Looking off toward the foot of the hill.)* You'd better decide quickly. They'll soon reach the carriage and discover I'm gone. Then all of Came-

	lot will be searching for me. At least *that* will be exciting. Unless of course everyone in Camelot is like you, and they all go home to deliberate.
Arthur:	*(Thrown off balance, enamoured, captivated, and overcome by a great sense of inadequacy.)* Oh, why isn't Merlyn here! He usually senses when I need him and appears. Why does he fail me now?
Guenevere:	Who?
Arthur:	Merlyn. My teacher. He would know immediately what to do. I'm not accomplished at thinking, so I have Merlyn do it for me. He's the wisest man alive. He lives backwards.
Guenevere:	I beg your pardon?
Arthur:	He lives backwards. He doesn't age. He youthens. He can remember the future so he can tell you what you'll be doing in it. Do you understand? *(She comes towards him. He never takes his eyes off her, as the wonder of her comes nearer.)*
Guenevere:	*(Now at ease.)* Of course I don't understand. But if you mean he's some sort of fortune-teller, I'd give a year in Paradise to know mine. I can never return to my own castle, and I absolutely refuse to go on to that one.
Arthur:	You refuse to go on—ever?
Guenevere:	Ever. My only choice is . . . Don't stare. It's rude. Who are you?
Arthur:	*(After a thought.)* Actually, they call me Wart.
Guenevere:	Wart? What a ridiculous name. Are you sure you heard them properly?
Arthur:	It's a nickname. It was given to me when I was a boy.
Guenevere:	You're rather sweet, in spite of your name. And I didn't think I'd like anyone in Camelot. Imagine riding seven hours in a carriage on the verge of hysteria, then seeing that horrible castle rising in the distance, and running away; then having a man plop from a tree like an overripe apple—you must admit for my first day

away from home it's quite a plateful. If only I
were not alone. Wart, why don't you . . . Is it
really Wart?

Arthur: Yes.

Guenevere: Wart, why don't you run away with me? *(Suddenly excited by the notion.)*

Arthur: I? Run away with you?

Guenevere: Of course. As my protector. Naturally, I would
be brutalized by strangers. I expect that. But it
would be dreadful if there were no one to rescue me. Think of it! We can travel the world.
France, Scotland, Spain . . .

Arthur: What a dream you spin, and how easily I
could be caught up in it. But I can't, Milady.
To serve as your protector would satisfy the
prayers of the most fanatic cavalier alive. But I
must decline.

Guenevere: *(Angry.)* You force me to stay?

Arthur: Not at all.

Guenevere: But you know you're the only one I know in
Camelot. Whom else can I turn to?

Arthur: Milady, if you persist in escaping, I'll find
someone trustworthy and brave to accompany
you.

Guenevere: Then do so immediately. There's not much
time.

Appendix B

Sample Auditions Material

Sample guidelines for auditioning for admission to one national theatre conservatory.

A Word about Auditions

Our auditions place special emphasis on the applicant's potential for future growth. We believe that imagination, personal initiative, self-discipline, stamina, seriousness of commitment to the legitimate stage, and trainability are fundamental.

By "trainability" we mean that we attempt to judge the applicant's potential for growth. We believe that this potential can be assessed by evaluating the student's ability to focus personal energies in a relaxed manner, which will enhance communicaiton of the conflict the character faces in the context of the play. Students who get trapped in "characterization" or "style" tend to demonstrate their level of virtuosity rather than to tap their deeper, inner resources.

Prepare *two* selections from plays, involving characters suitable to your age and experience.

1. Choose selections from plays. Poems are not acceptable. Do not memorize one-character monologues from one-man shows such as "Mark Twain Tonight" or "The Belle of Amherst."

Courtesy of The Goodman Theatre.

2. Do not use dialects or singing. We recommend that you do not use pieces from classical literature that require advanced work in the analysis of metered verse.
3. Only one character should be represented in each selection.
4. The total time for both selections together should not be more than four minutes. No introductory material is necessary.
5. Your selection must be memorized.
6. The group work will entail vigorous activity to involve the whole body. We suggest that you do not eat for at least two hours before the audition.

Sample college audition notice

Production Audition Information

The attached reprint* of an article published in the American Theatre Association *Theatre News* is provided for your information and assistance. Its purpose is to help you, not intimidate you. If you find ideas there you do not really understand, don't worry about them but make use of anything which does suggest how you might approach the business of "trying out" for a show. Our students find that developing a good audition technique may take a long time. As you continue to participate in auditions you will no doubt find more of the information in this article helpful and sensible. We encourage you to grow as an auditionee through participating in not just one but many auditions.

We would make the following recommendations for auditioning for theatre productions:

---

*This sample notice is normally distributed and posted with an attached guideline sheet, not included in this Appendix.

Courtesy of Hope College Theatre, Holland, Michigan.

1. Use material close to your own age and type. Something from a role you have already performed is often an excellent choice, since you will already have done considerable work on the piece. At the same time, we encourage you to be imaginative in your selection. Poetic and prose (short story, novel) works may furnish material as interesting as dramatic works.
2. We prefer a prepared audition piece, memorized. If you do not have such a piece, however, we encourage you to come anyway—even for only a "cold" reading. The more prepared your material is, the easier it is for our directors to determine your suitability for a particular role. But if you are not here presenting *some* kind of audition, they obviously have no opportunity to consider you at all!

We will try to provide whatever assistance is possible to the novice auditionee. Please do not hesitate to ask us to clarify anything in the procedure you do not understand, or just to help you overcome those audition jitters. We can at least say to you: "Yes, we know. Everyone goes through this trauma. We've been there ourselves."

Please note, finally, that auditions are open to the entire campus community. Although on occasion we must provide specific opportunities for performance majors, intention to major in theatre is not a prerequisite for being cast in a show.

Coach's checklist for auditioning

1. Did the actor warm up, so that his voice projects well in the space and his movements seem alert and responsive?
2. Does the introduction to the audition display confidence and a sense of professionalism, and is it minimal?
3. Is the actor relaxed and comfortable speaking informally about himself and his interests?
4. Does the actor have the appropriate age and physical characteristics for the role?

5. Is each audition piece complete in the sense of having a beginning, middle, and end?

6. Does it seem like the actor is born to play this character, or is he or she just very well-prepared with it?

7. Is the actor relaxed, comfortable, and having fun with the audition?

8. Is the actor using furniture and hand props effectively, both in setting-up beforehand as well as during the performance?

9. Is the actor trying to "blow the auditors out of the room" or is he or she acting and reacting honestly?

10. Does the audition open out to the audience for communication and contact or does it seem tight, inhibited, and confined in the space?

11. Is it clear what the actor is fighting for in the scene?

12. Is there a sense of urgency and importance to the scene?

13. Is the actor clear about the physical location of his or her vis-à-vis and is he or she effectively using the imaginary character to propel the speech?

14. Is the actor playing the events and discoveries clearly?

15. Does the actor understand the piece and use everything the material contains?

16. Has the actor displayed a range of skills, eliminated any personal mannerisms, and presented variety in the total audition?

17. Is the actor's costume loose and comfortable enough to permit him to perform the audition in a relaxed and controlled manner, and does the costume display the actor's good taste and sense of self-respect?

18. Is the actor flexible enough to add a different emotion, change one or two major goals, or alter the relationship slightly when asked to perform the audition a second time?

Sample of an "Auditions Tip Sheet" published by the Michigan Theatre Association, in connection with annual midwestern region auditions.

Here are some things to think about when you are preparing for the audition.

A. *Preparation*

1. Select appropriate pieces. They should be contrasting pieces, but not necessarily Shakespeare. Suit the selections to the types of theatres and productions for which you are auditioning.

2. Choose pieces that are within your character range. Try to stick with pieces that you have done before and with which you are comfortable. Untried pieces seldom work well. Remember that good dramatic material can help to sell your skills to prospective employers.

3. Pick a song that fits and shows your range. Don't do overdone selections. Eight bars is sufficient. Have more ready to go for callbacks.

4. Avoid weird or overdone selections, or selections not easily represented in a short speech (Maggie the cat, Blanche, Alan Strang, Starbuck).

5. Your selections should be fully memorized. No scripts!

6. Don't have someone come in and read with you. Do a selection that works as a monologue, or patch together several short speeches which are logically consistent.

7. Time your pieces. Stay within the limit. In general, be too short rather than too long.

This tip sheet was prepared by Cynthia A. Ballard, Kellogg Community College, Battle Creek, Michigan with the help of James Knox, The Barn Theatre, Augusta, Michigan, and Roger Ellis, President of the Michigan Theatre Association.

8. If you plan to use a tape recording for your musical number, practice with it. It should be of the best quality you can afford. Know how to work the tape machine. It will be to your advantage to practice with the equipment.

9. Practice your audition from beginning to end including your introduction. Practice in front of a group of people to get reactions, and work with a coach.

10. Fill out the audition forms completely, including the important points of your resume. Often that is all the theatre has to look at until you present your full resume at an interview. Fill in accurate availability dates. Use a typewriter.

11. Try to find out something about the theatres for which you are auditioning.

12. Make your resume as impressive as possible. Look for examples of the professional resume. It should be one page, neatly typed. Be honest about roles you have played and about your union affiliations. Have available some references with phone numbers and addresses. Ask those people if they would mind recommending you. Remember that your resume can help to sell you, once you've left the audition.

13. Get a good night's sleep. That's better than cramming. Get up early to prepare.

14. Be careful what you eat and drink before an audition!

15. Most of all, be positive about the experience. Look on the audition as further experience and as beneficial in and of itself. And remember that the worst that could happen is that you won't get the job you already don't have!

B. *The Performance*

1. Arrive early to warm up and acquaint yourself with the audition area.

2. The right clothing is *very important*. Visual identification is important to make you stand out. Strong, solid colors make a statement. Look your best!
   a. Women should wear skirts or dresses; if dancers, dance attire.
   b. Juvenile and young leading men should wear dance attire or simple shirt and pants and/or sweater.
   c. Character men should wear a sports jacket and sweater or suit and tie.
   d. Pay attention to your hair. Have an attractive hairdo.
   e. Avoid clutter. No coins in pockets or jangling bracelets or keys.
   f. Use basic stage makeup but not too much. Eyes are important.
   g. Wear the right shoes. Clogs are rather noisy! Wear shoes that help you to move well.

3. Remember that you start your audition from the moment that you enter. Sell yourself from start to finish. Remember also that in addition to the stage characters you present in your monologues, the other "character" you'll present is yourself!

4. Clearly state your name and number at the beginning of the audition.

5. You don't need a great deal of introduction. Don't go into the story of the whole play.

6. Try not to take too long to "get into character." You'll go over your time limit.

7. Do your best piece first. Do your song first or second so you are sure to get it in.

8. Try not to make a major production out of costumes or props. *You* are auditioning, not your special effects.

9. Don't ask the musician to transpose music. Make it as easy as possible for the accompanist and your audition will be more successful.

10. Be simple and direct. Don't be static, yet don't block an entire scene.

11. Don't begin by apologizing for your material. It's a bad start.

12. Find your light and take the stage.

13. Keep your volume up.

14. Keep within the time limit. Stop when the timer indicates your time is up.

15. Relate to the audience as a group. Don't ignore them. Communicate with them and share with them.

16. Your attitude should be positive, but not offensive.

17. Make a strong exit. Thank the producers and make no apologies either by word or body!

C. *The Interview*

1. Have copies of your resume and pictures available for the theatres. Photos should be 8½ × 11 inches, stapled to the back of your resume. Black-and-white glossy prints only.

2. Push your technical skills, too. Many theatres need multifaceted theatre people.

3. If you get called back by a theatre and you don't plan to interview, leave some message so they don't wait for you.

4. If a theatre makes an offer or gives you an application, you should send some reply to them even if you decide not to accept.

5. Ask questions in the interview. Theatres have different requirements and working conditions. Remember, if it isn't in the contract, you ain't-a-gonna get it. So be sure you know all the details before you leave.

6. Be honest about what you want out of this theater experience. It will help both the theatre and you to decide to accept or not to accept a position offered.

7. Have a "verbal resume" rehearsed, so that you can talk confidently with producers about your experience.

These are just a few hints to help you make it through the auditioning experience.

Break-a-leg!

Sample resume

Peter Zelaske
Actor-Tech

96 Wentworth Ave.
Big Falls, IL 60721
312-733-0279
312-773-4496

Height: 5'10"
Weight: 172 lb.
Hair: Brown
Eyes: Gray
Age range: 18-22
Singing range: bass

Stage

Peter	Zoo Story	Northwestern University
Simon	Caucasian Chalk Circle	Northwestern University
Truffaldino	Servant of Two Masters	Northwestern University
Benvolio	Romeo and Juliet	Court Theatre, Chicago
Tranio	Taming of the Shrew	Court Theatre (with Erica Davies)
Mr. Rich	Celebration	Northwestern University
Tuschenbach	Three Sisters	Southern Illinois University, Carbondale
Hummel	Basic Training of Pavlo Hummell	Southern Illinois University, Carbondale

TV/Film

criminal, victims, witnesses	3 crime stoppers TV-film spots	Springfield Police Dept.
mime/dancer	video dance concert	Southern Illinois University Grad Film Dept.
Ralph, jealous husband	original student teleplay	Northwestern Grad Film Dept.

Skills

Dance—4 years, modern/tap/jazz/choreography; Northwestern University
Singing—class voice 2 years/choir and choral 11 years; high school/university
Makeup—cosmetology program 1 year; Truman College, Chicago
Crew chief/stage manager—7 plays, 1 dance concert; Southern Illinois University and Northwestern University
Voice—Lessac summer workshop, 6 weeks

Training

Acting: Improv, characterization, voice (2 classes), scene study, mime (2 years); Acting for cameras	Northwestern University Southern Illinois University
Stagecraft: Scene construction, lighting, audio	Southern Illinois University
Combatives: company workshops, 8 weeks	Court Theatre, Chicago
Period Dance: company workshops, 8 weeks	Court Theatre, Chicago
TV commercials: class, 12 weeks	Audition Centre, Chicago

206

Sample of actors' tax deductions

1. Union Dues	
2. Talent Directory	
3. Trade & Casting Periodicals	
4. Booking, Agent & Personal Management Fees	
5. Research & Reference Materials Used in the Profession	
6. Courses and Lessons Related to the Profession	
Vocal & Music	
Acting	
Dance	
7. Music, Study Records & Drama Material	
8. Professional Photos and Resumes	
9. Professional Wardrobe (usable for performances only)	
10. Cleaning & Laundry of Professional Wardrobe	
11. Theatrical Make-Up (including wigs)	
12. Telephone	
Answering Service	
Outside Telephone	
Home Telephone (excess units & long distance)	
13. Audition Tapes	
14. Musical & Special Arrangements	
15. Theater Tickets for Promotion & Study	
16. Professional Fees (Legal, Accounting, Tax Preparation)	
*17. Entertainment Expense	
18. Postage, Flowers & Xmas Cards	
19. Office Supplies	
20. Local Transportation	
Auto Mileage	

Sample of actors' tax deductions (cont'd)

Less % Personal Use			
Total Business Auto - 1st 15,000 mi. @ 20¢ then 11¢ per mile thereafter			
Parking & Tolls			
Bus & Taxi Cabs			
21. Rent Allocation as Professional Studio & Office			
(Taxpayer rents a _____ room apartment of which _____ room(s) is exclusively for an Office & Studio.)			
Rent			
Utilities			
Insurance			
Sub-total			
*22. Travel Away from Home (Plane, Train, Auto, etc.)			
*23. Meals & Lodging Away from Home			
24. Transportation to and from Engagements & Airports			
25. Tips			
26. Musical Instrument Cartage			
27. Musical Instrument Insurance			
28. Musical Instrument Repairs			
29. Musical Instrument Upkeep & Supplies			
30. Paid Substitutes & Standbys			
31. Depreciation of Instruments & Professional Equipment (See Schedule)			
32. Miscellaneous & Sundry			
Total Expenses			

*To be deductible, records must be kept indicating time, place and amount of expenditure, person(s) involved including business relationship, and business purpose.

Appendix C

Reference Books and Manuals

Books on the acting business

The following list contains the most valuable and up-to-date books describing both the nature of the acting business and the methods professionals must use in order to find work. They cover films, television, and the stage, and they deal with the major industry centers of New York and Los Angeles, as well as with certain aspects of regional theatre.

Bayer, William. *Breaking Through, Selling Out, Dropping Dead, and Other Notes on Filmmaking.* New York: Delta, 1973. Covers the southern California scene vividly and with humor by someone who knows what he's talking about.

Cohen, Robert. *Acting Professionally,* 3d ed. Palo Alto, Calif.: Mayfield, 1981. The most straightforward, accurate, and honest description of what the acting business is like in the United States and what it takes to break into it. An absolute must for any student-actor seriously contemplating the possibility of entering this dismal and indescribably wonderful profession.

Craig, David. *On Singing Onstage.* New York: Macmillan, 1978. By anyone's standards, the most inclusive, detailed, and knowledgeable handbook on how to prepare and audition songs. Requires experience in singing, acting, and dramatic auditioning.

Finchlevy, Joan. *Audition! A Complete Guide for Actors, with an Annotated Selection of Readings.* New York: Prentice-Hall,

1984. Contains the most recent listings of play selections from the contemporary theatre.

Fridell, Squire. *Acting in Television Commercials for Fun and Profit.* New York: Crown, 1980. Don't be put off by the simplistic title. The book will satisfy anyone's basic curiosity about this "bread and butter" sector of the industry, which accounts for the major portion of all income for actors who work in film, in television, or on the stage.

Hunt, Gordon. *How to Audition.* New York: Harper and Row, 1977. Contains interviews with numerous celebrities on the auditions process and tips on how to prepare scenes. Good reading for undergraduate students, although the acting methods are more suitable for experienced professionals.

Jessup, Cortland, and Alpert S. Lee. *The Actor's Guide to Breaking into Commercials.* New York: Pilot, 1980. Very informative and up-to-date as a survey of this aspect of the profession. Remember that special schools and workshops geared specifically to acting in commercials are absolutely essential and that a book by itself can be of only limited value as a survey.

Logan, Tom. *How to Act and Eat at the Same Time.* Washington, D.C.: Communications Press, 1982. Like the Cohen book, a required manual for breaking in. Up-to-date figures and complete information, but no treatment of acting methods for preparing audition material.

———. *Acting in the Million Dollar Minute: The Art and Business of Performing in TV Commercials.* Washington, D.C.: Communications Press, 1984. Contains the most up-to-date figures and facts on this sector of the acting marketplace.

Markus, Tom. *The Professional Actor.* New York: Drama Book Specialists, 1979. An excellent book for student actors. Surveys the field of stage acting and outlines the methods for selling oneself eventually in the professional marketplace. Written by an actor-director with the needs of students in mind.

Matson, Katinka. *The Working Actor.* New York: Penguin, 1976. Like the books by Robert Cohen and Tom Markus, this, too, stresses the business side of the acting profession. Written from a woman's point of view, it is very readable, although the figures and statistics are now out of date. The author is an actress and casting director.

McNoughton, Robert, and Bruce McNoughton. *Act Now: An Actor's Guide for Breaking In*. Hollywood, Calif.: Global, 1982. An outstanding and up-to-date perspective on stage and film acting, dealing especially with young actors. Emphasizes how an acting career is possible and describes several avenues for young actors to take.

Nahas, Rebecca. *Your Acting Career: How to Break into and Survive in the Theatre*. New York: Crown, 1976. Another book on the business methods and practical problems the working professional must handle in order to pursue a career. Extremely readable, it is written from a female point of view and is fully professional in outlook and in background. Facts and figures are somewhat dated.

Shurtleff, Michael. *Audition*. New York: Walker, 1980. A book on professional stage acting, with suggested "methods" for approaching cold readings and scenes. The most widely used auditions book on the market, it was written by America's most famous and successful casting director. Tends to emphasize the "method" approach to acting. An absolute *must* for all student actors and fine general reading for anyone.

Anthologies of scenes and monologues

The following books vary widely in terms of their inclusiveness and timeliness. Some may be inaccessible to you or to your school library, but all contain good selections for class work. Several contain up-to-date, exciting, and little-used material.

Bell, Richard O., and Joan Kuder. *Auditions and Scenes from Shakespeare*. Boulder, Colo.: Armado and Moth, 1984. A 175-page directory of 700 selections from the entire Shakespearean dramatic canon. Each directory listing provides the number of male-female actors, approximate time length, suggestions for editing, and synopsis.

Grumbach, Jane, and Robert Emerson. *Actor's Guide to Monologues.* 2 vols. New York: Drama Book Specialists, 1974.
———. *Actor's Guide to Scenes,* 2 vols. New York: Drama Book Specialists, 1973. These four pamphlets are indexes that list only the selection and where to find it. They do not contain the pieces themselves. Very helpful for library work, the listings are broken down into categories: sex, age, comic/serious style, classical, and modern.
———. *Monologues: Men,* 2 vols. New York: Drama Book Specialists, 1976.
———. *Monologues: Women,* 2 vols. New York: Drama Book Specialists, 1976. These four paperbacks contain actual pieces. The selections are good, although not all of them are within the average age range of undergraduate students. All the selections are contemporary and some are little used.

Handman, Wynn. *Modern American Scenes for Student Actors.* New York: Bantam, 1978. All the selections are contemporary in this paperback, which also contains good monologues. The monologues are frequently done at auditions, but all the material is excellent and exciting for studio and rehearsal work.

Olfson, Lewy. *Fifty Great Scenes for Student Actors.* New York: Bantam, 1970. Somewhat dated, but if you can obtain a copy it will give you some good selections for studio work and rehearsals.

Price, Jonathan. *Classic Scenes.* New York: Mentor, 1979. This is a widely used book for scene-study classes in period drama and is a must for auditions requiring classical material. Selections are indexed at the back according to sex and number of characters. There is also another helpful index according to acting problems for rehearsal explorations. For some reason, Christopher Marlowe is listed in the contents as "Master S." but don't let that discourage you.

Rudnicki, Stefan. *Classical Monologues,* 4 vols. New York: Drama Book Specialists, 1979-82. These, too, are for work in period drama; all deal with Renaissance authors.

Schulman, Michael, and Eva Mekler. *Contemporary Scenes for Student Actors.* New York: Penguin, 1980. As the title indicates, this paperback contains only modern scenes; but the first fourteen pages present the most valuable and practical approach to acting scenes that can be found anywhere. The selections are within the age range of undergraduates, and each contains a brief introduction for rehearsal purposes.

Seto, Judith R. *The Young Actors' Workbook.* New York: Grove, 1984. An excellent up-to-date book containing fifty scenes and monologues with character descriptions, plot synopses, and descriptions of settings. For studio rehearsal work and for auditions material.

Videotape

Blanchard, Nina. "How to Break into Motion Pictures, Television, Commercials, and Modeling." Hollywood, Calif.: Anthony Productions, 1985. (Address: Anthony Productions, P.O. Box 708, Hollywood, Calif., 90028.) Consists of tips and illustrations, and interviews with actors, coaches, and casting directors. Very solid, informative, and current.

Notes

Chapter one: Introduction

1. A demographic profile of students in training at San Francisco's American Conservatory Theatre, one of the nation's foremost acting-training programs, tends to validate this conclusion. For example, out of eighty three students enrolled during the 1977-78 session, 57 percent had earned college degrees and 90 percent had a minimum of two years of college. In order to become a candidate for their professional degree, the M.F.A., all students are required to have completed a four-year B.A. or B.S. degree program.

2. B.J. Jones, A.T.A. Region III Conference, Chicago, 27 September 1980.

3. Quoted in Selma Jean Cohen, *Dance as a Theatre Art* (New York: Dodd, Mead, 1975), 139.

4. Michael Shurtleff, *Audition* (New York: Walker, 1978), 104, 157.

Chapter two: The auditions context

1. The terms "closed" and "open" are also used to refer to tryouts that are open to everyone who wishes to attend, or closed to all who are not enrolled as students (or professionally, closed to nonunion actors).

2. "The Goodman School's Dramatic Resurgence," *Chicago Tribune Magazine*, 23 March 1980, 35.

3. Tom Markus, *The Professional Actor* (New York: Drama Book Specialists, 1979), 34.

4. Michael Shurtleff, *Audition* (New York: Walker, 1978), 19.

5. In the San Francisco Bay area, for example, where I first began my training, some now famous professional theatres began as outgrowths of college drama programs: the Actors Workshop, the Berkeley Repertory Theatre, the Magic Theatre, the Berkeley Stage Company, and others.

6. Salaries for summer work vary widely across the country. In 1980 to 1982, they ranged from $40 to $275 per week, with $100 a little better than average. Many theatres offer low-cost company housing and other incentives as part of the employment package.

7. I use the example of *Hamlet* because I'm quite certain that no student in his right mind would ever, under any circumstances, prepare one of those soliloquies as an audition.

8. ATA Region III Conference, Chicago, 27 September 1980. Author's notes.

9. Uta Hagen recommends actors to have at least thirty pieces "ready to go" for any occasion, and this is fairly standard among professional working actors (Chicago acting workshop, 12 February 1982).

10. It is almost always inadvisable to prepare a scene for summer theatre work from a play that will be done by the producing group. You narrow your chances in two ways by doing so: either the directors will already have cast the major parts or they will see you in only one role and thus tend to overlook your suitability for other parts.

11. Kirk Frederick, producer-director of Cameo Productions, San Francisco, interview, 29 December 1981.

12. Robert Goldsby, founding director, Berkeley Stage Company, interview, 2 January 1981.

13. Markus, *Professional Actor*, 21-22.

14. Moshe Feldenkrais, *The Elusive Obvious*, or *Basic Feldenkrais* (Cupertino, Calif.: Meta, 1981), xi-xii. The Feldenkrais

"technique" is an intensive body-mind training approach that is taught all over the world. It is one of the most important movement training methods for actors and is used on an ongoing basis in most acting-training conservatories in the United States.

15. Robert Cohen, *Theatre* (Palo Alto: Mayfield, 1981), 327.

16. Eric Morris and Joan Hotchkis, *No Acting Please* (Los Angeles, Calif.: Whitehouse/Spelling, 1979), 68.

17. Interview, 11 February 1982.

18. Charles Marowitz, *The Method as Means* (London: Jenkins, 1961), 42.

19. Eric Morris, one of Hollywood's most recognized acting teachers, has developed an interesting type of life-study exercise called "Farmer's Market" in which he guides students to observe according to eight criteria:

   a. How is your subject dressed?
   b. What props are your subjects using and how do they relate to these objects?
   c. What degree of involvement do you observe between your subjects and their activities or their companions?
   d. How aware is your subject with regard to his or her physicality? The weather? The place? The social context?
   e. Do you observe your subject outwardly expressing one thing while inwardly feeling something very different ("compensating" by superimposing a socially acceptable exterior over one's real feelings)?
   f. What does your subject seem to be self-conscious about and how does your subject seem to handle this self-consciousness?
   g. How does your subject eat and what philosophical or psychological attitudes can you deduce on the basis of your observation?
   h. To what "decade" does your subject belong, judging from your observations in the other seven categories? Can you see your subject "walking out of a 1947 calendar or a 1950 movie magazine"? What point in history was probably "the most exciting time of life for

him . . . the point where his curiosity died and the striving to grow ended"? *No Acting Please* (Los Angeles, Calif.: Whitehouse/Spelling, 1979), 51-54.

20. I was once privileged to witness the famous mime Bobby Shields get slugged to the pavement in San Francisco by an indignant passerby who caught Shields mimicking his walk and body language. Before he became commercially successful, Shields used to entertain lunch-hour visitors in Union Square by doing improv routines and life studies, passing the hat around afterwards.

Chapter three: Selecting audition material

1. Louis John Dezseran, *The Student Actor's Handbook* (Palo Alto: Mayfield, 1975), 196. A sample cover sheet for the U.R.T.A. auditions is reprinted in the appendix of this book. U.R.T.A. is one organization you will hear more about if you choose to continue in a professional direction. In order to transfer from your college or university into a conservatory or graduate school, you will have to demonstrate your abilities at national auditions conducted by U.R.T.A. (T.C.G. auditions were discontinued in 1981). There will be preliminary auditions in your state that will screen out the candidates of little potential before recommending the best auditionees to the national auditions in selected cities. There the representatives from theatre schools to which you've applied or from producing theatres looking for new company members will audition you in the finals and make their decisions.

2. I realize that many educational theatre directors are often forced to cast students in roles that are radically different from their actual ages, but I am speaking here of pieces you select for trying out. If a director wants you to read for a ninety-year-old hermaphrodite with green hair at the tryouts, however, go right ahead and do it.

3. Tom Markus, *The Professional Actor* (New York: Drama Book Specialists, 1979), 42.

4. Many acting coaches will point this out to new students entering auditions because directors are constantly evaluating auditionees from the first moment they appear. In his
professional acting handbook, Tom Markus describes the
whole audition process as a scene in itself, assigning acting
objectives to each part for a good overall performance: "First,
you must arrive at the audition hall. . . . The second part of
your audition performance is your entrance. . . . The third
part of your audition is the interview proper. . . . The fourth
part of your audition performance will comprise the presentation. . . . Your fifth and final part is your exit" *(The Professional Actor*, 36-43).

5. Quoted in Dennis Powers, "You're too fat . . . You're
too thin . . . You remind me of my first wife . . . Thank you
and goodbye," *Playbill* (Los Angeles), January 1984, 10.

6. Michael Leibert, Artistic Director, Berkeley Repertory
Theatre, interview, 29 December 1981.

7. Monte Davis, Milwaukee Repertory Theatre, interview, 17 September 1980.

8. A sample college audition notice of this nature ap-
pears in the appendix.

9. *The Working Actor* (New York: Penguin, 1976), 26.

10. *Seven Keys to Baldpate* (New York: American Play Co.,
1941).

11. *Danton's Death*, tr. William I. Oliver, acting version
University of California, Berkeley, 1972.

12. *Commanche Cafe* (New York: Samuel French, 1977).

Chapter four: Preparing audition pieces

1. Robert Goldsby, interview, 1 February 1982.

2. Liv Ullmann, *Changing* (New York: Knopf, 1977), 96-
97.

3. "How to Approach a Scene," in *Contemporary Scenes
for Student Actors*, edited by Michael Schulman and Eva Mekler
(New York: Penguin, 1980), 27.

4. Quoted from the film *Borrowed Faces* (New York: McGraw-Hill, 1979).

5. Aaron Frankel, interview, 3 May 1982.

6. William James, University of Santa Clara, interview, 18 December 1981.

7. This approach was first suggested to me by William Oliver, director and dramaturg for San Francisco's One-Act Theatre Company, who decried the blunt, "plosive," monotone that so many young American actors seem to have adopted as their "style." He leads actors towards more musical speech patterns and broader range and variety in their inflections by twisting the sounds of individual words and phrases.

8. A more advanced version of this exercise is the method recommended by Arthur Lessac, one of America's most prestigious voice teachers. The Lessac "system" may already be a part of your school's program, or you will certainly encounter it if you continue professionally. You might look at his textbook to see how vowel and consonant rehearsal can be used for interpreting speeches: *The Use and Training of the Human Voice* (New York: Drama Book Specialists, 1967), 182-206.

9. This exercise is used by Broadway director Aaron Frankel in his classes on acting Shakespeare (interview, 3 May 1982).

10. Uta Hagen, *Respect for Acting* (New York: Macmillan, 1973), 122-23. An excellent chapter devoted to monologues in this book is entitled "Talking to Yourself" (119-23). Although some of Hagen's rehearsal methods are best taught in a long-term class, there are a few valuable hints in this chapter for auditions preparation.

11. Michael Shurtleff, *Audition* (New York: Walker, 1978), 53, 66-67.

12. Angela Paton, interview, 2 January 1982.

13. I have phrased these general guidelines positively, though many pages could be written listing "what not to do" during an audition. One of the handiest checklists for move-

ment problems is provided by James Penrod of the University of California, Irvine, *Movement for the Performing Artist* (Palo Alto: Mayfield, 1974), 149. Compare pages 133-51 in his chapter entitled "Developing the Role Through Movement."

14. Eric Morris and Joan Hotchkis, *No Acting Please* (Los Angeles, Calif.: Whitehouse/Spelling, 1979), 174.

15. William Redfield, *Letters from an Actor* (New York: Viking, 1967), p. 59.

16. Robert Goldsby, interview, 2 January 1982.

17. Quoted in David Nicolette, "Versatile Actor Cariou Has Best of Two Worlds," *Grand Rapids Press* (Michigan), 25 April 1982, p. 3H.

18. Paul Muni, "The Mechanics of Movie Acting," in Toby Cole and Helen Krich Chinoy, *Actors on Acting* (New York: Crown, 1962), p. 529. Numerous untrained performers recruited for TV and films frequently point out how important proper training is in order to remain in the business after one or two roles. Nastassia Kinski, who was Roman Polanski's twenty-one-year-old "starlet" in *Tess of the D'Urbervilles* and also did *Cat People* for Paul Schrader, says, "I'm very frustrated when I make a movie, because it's always bits and pieces that I have to bring out of instinct and intuition. But because I don't have the best technique I will often lose something in rehearsal that I want to do again in front of the camera. So I need theatrical technique in order to learn how to get it back whenever I want it, to be able to do the same thing again and again." Nastassia Kinski interview with Gene Siskel in the *Chicago Tribune*, 4 April 1982, Sec. 6, 25.

19. Aaron Frankel, interview, 5 March 1982.

20. Robert Goldsby, interview, 2 January 1982.

21. Judy Jenkins, interview, 4 March 1982.

22. Robert Cohen, *Acting Professionally* (Palo Alto, Calif.: Mayfield, 1981), 87.

23. James Roose-Evans, interview, 12 July 1980.

24. Jack Fletcher, interview, 4 January 1982.

25. Auditon workship at ACTF Region III—East, Kalamazoo, Mich., 6 January 1984.

Chapter five: The audition

1. This method was explained by Aaron Frankel in his audition class at the Herbert Berghof Studio, New York, 4 March 1982.

2. Aaron Frankel, *Writing the Broadway Musical* (New York: Drama Book Specialists, 1977), 20.

3. Jack Fletcher, American Conservatory Theatre, 4 January 1982.

4. Mary Anne McGarry, Riverside Shakespeare Company, New York, 1 March 1982.

5. *Stanislavsky on the Art of the Stage*, tr. David Magarshack (New York: Hill and Wang, 1961), 149, italics mine.

6. "Physical Action as a Means to an End," *Stanislavsky's Legacy*, edited and translated by Elizabeth R. Hapgood (New York: Theatre Arts, 1968), 46.

7. Interview, Goodman School, Chicago, 8 October 1982.

8. Darryl Hickman, producer, quoted in Gordon Hunt, *How to Audition* (New York: Harper and Row, 1977), 259.

9. Robert Goldsby interview, 2 January 1982.

Chapter six: Musical theatre

1. Aaron Frankel, *Writing the Broadway Musical* (New York: Drama Book Specialists, 1977), 19.

2. Michael Shurtleff, *Audition* (New York: Walker, 1978), 146. The only exception to this "triple threat" requirement is the rare possibility that the director will also be casting performers who can only sing ("pit singers" who are located with the orchestra to help the stage actors with choral numbers) or who can only dance (also an occasional option with some directors).

3. Robert Cohen, *Acting Professionally* (Palo Alto, Calif.: Mayfield, 1981), 24.

4. Shurtleff, *Audition*, 145.

5. David Craig makes a strong Shakespearean connection when he remarks that show songs are really "soliloquies" and points out that "most actors would be almost as pleased to appear in a musical as they would a play of Shakespeare's." *On Singing Onstage* (New York: Macmillan, 1978), xxii.

6. *The Boy Friend* (New York: Chappell Music Co., Inc.). Used by permission.

7. Robert Peterson, interview, 6 May 1982.

8. Hal Prince, *Contradictions: Notes on Twenty-Six Years in the Theatre* (New York: Dodd, Mead, 1974), 150.

9. "The Auditions Game," *Dramatics*, Mar. 1982., 46, italics mine.

10. Frankel, *Writing the Broadway Musical*, 81-82.

11. Fred Silver, New York coach in musical auditioning and performance technique, urges seven "rules of thumb" for auditionees, summarized here: "(1) Never select a song to perform that is better than you are. . . . (2) Select material you are prepared to 'live with' for a long, long time. . . . (3) Find songs that allow you to act 'who' you are. . . . If you don't think you can say it as a monologue without having egg on your face, then don't sing it. . . . (4) Make the song a complete scene. . . . (5) Use all your acting techniques in mounting the song. . . . With a song, all one's acting techniques are restricted and controlled by the tempo of the music and the speed at which the lyric's delivered. (6) Make the lyric come alive. . . . (7) Find a key for the song that suits your vocal range. There is no such thing as an 'original key' for an audition song." More complete details on these guidelines can be found in Silver's article "Audition Doctor," *Backstage* (New York), 26 November 1982, 46-71.

12. As with dramatic auditions, coaching for song auditions can be obtained in many major cities around the country. Unquestionably the best song training for actors is conducted in Los Angeles by David Craig, whose book *On Singing Onstage* has already been referred to. The book is valuable reading for student actors and collegiate coaches, but it does presuppose that the actor have a sound basis in acting and singing experience.

13. In his workshop techniques, David Craig recommends that students maintain as much objective distance from "the song" as possible when doing literal paraphrase. He suggests avoiding the first-person pronoun completely and instead say "This is a story about . . ." or "She says that. . . ." In Craig's terms, the student wants to produce "a piece of reportage. Be prepared to defend it if challenged, and know that the defense must rest in the stated lyric and not in what you have imagined or assumed it to say" (*On Singing Onstage,* 136).

14. From *The Boy Friend* by Sandy Wilson (New York: Chappell Music Co., Inc.). Used by permission. Interlinear paraphrase taken from a student project in my workshop.

15. Stephen Sondheim, Copyright 1970. The Herald Square Music Co. and Rilting Music, Inc. Used by permission.

Chapter seven: Supporting material

1. Kirk Frederick, director of Cameo Productions and owner of Kirk Frederick Graphics, San Francisco, interview, 29 December 1981.

2. Gordon Hunt, *How to Audition* (New York: Harper and Row, 1977), 25.

3. In conversation with students in my auditions workshop, 17 September 1980.

4. In case you're interested, a sample list of tax-deductible expenses for actors is provided in the Appendix. You are eligible to take these deductions whenever you itemize your expenses on your tax return, either as a student or as a "working" actor. Check the Internal Revenue Service if you're unsure about all this.

5. Does your theatre department give yearly scholarships, prizes, or other academic awards? Does the faculty assist promising seniors with assembling their portfolios, preparing applications, resumes, and the like? Then talk to your professor or your department chairman to skim a few bucks off the operating budget in order to sponsor a promising

student like yourself. After all, you will be representing the department after you leave. And a "talent grant" or "prize" for the best students is often a standard feature in many schools.

6. Interview, 3 March 1982.

7. Kim Garfield, "Producer Michael Stuart Holds 'Nine' the Auditions," *DramaLogue*, 45 (Nov. 11, 1982), 7.

8. Robert Cohen, *Acting Professionally* (Palo Alto, Calif.: Mayfield, 1981), 15.

9. Baldridge, interview, 3 March 1982.

10. In workshop session, 12 February 1982.

11. Aaron Frankel, interview, 4 March 1982.

12. Interview on the "Dick Cavett Show," 19 October 1981.

13. B.J. Jones, ATA Region III Conference, Chicago, 27 September 1980.

14. Judy Jenkins, CBS casting, interview, 4 March 1982.

15. Quoted in Dwayne W. Dyer, *Pulling Your Own Strings* (New York: Avon, 1967), 36.

16. Eric Morris and Joan Hotchkis, *No Acting Please* (Los Angeles, Calif.: Whitehouse/Spelling, 1979), 15.

Index

Credits